Oyindamola Oluyemo

GUARDIANS OF THE DIGITAL FRONTIER

Advanced Strategies in AI and Cloud Security Defense

TABLE OF CONTENTS

PREFACE

The digital systems that support modern life are expanding at a pace that few industries have experienced before. Artificial intelligence now influences decision making, automation, and predictive analysis across sectors, while cloud computing has become the foundation for data storage, application deployment, and global collaboration. These advances have delivered speed, scale, and efficiency, but they have also introduced new forms of risk that traditional security approaches were not designed to manage. As cyber threats grow more adaptive and complex, the need for intelligent, resilient, and well governed security frameworks has become increasingly urgent.

This book was written in response to that reality. *Guardians of the Digital Frontier: Advanced Strategies in AI and Cloud Security Defense* examines how artificial intelligence and cloud technologies can be secured in a way that supports innovation without compromising trust, privacy, or operational stability. Rather than treating security as a separate or reactive function, this work approaches cybersecurity as an integrated discipline that must evolve alongside the systems it protects.

The motivation behind this book is grounded in both academic inquiry and real world observation. Many organizations continue to struggle with balancing rapid digital transformation against regulatory requirements, operational resilience, and growing threat exposure. Security frameworks often lag behind technological change, leaving gaps that adversaries are quick to exploit. At the same time, compliance efforts are frequently manual, fragmented, and difficult to sustain in dynamic environments. These challenges call for a shift in how cybersecurity is understood and implemented.

Artificial intelligence offers a powerful response to these challenges when applied with discipline and clarity. AI driven models enable continuous monitoring, adaptive defense, and data informed decision making at a scale that manual processes cannot achieve. When integrated properly into cloud security architecture, AI can improve visibility, strengthen governance, and support proactive threat mitigation. However, these capabilities also introduce new questions related to accountability, transparency, and risk management. This book addresses both the opportunities and the responsibilities that come with AI enabled security systems.

The structure of this work is designed to guide readers from foundational concepts to advanced applications. Early chapters establish core cybersecurity principles and explore how AI and cloud computing have reshaped the threat landscape. Subsequent sections examine practical defense strategies, resilient system design, data protection, and governance frameworks aligned with global standards. The later chapters look ahead, addressing emerging risks and the role of leadership in sustaining effective security programs over time.

A key objective of this book is to bridge theory and practice. The methodologies and frameworks discussed are supported by peer reviewed research, industry standards, and empirical analysis. At the same time, they are presented with an emphasis on applicability. Readers are encouraged to think critically about how these strategies can be adapted to their own environments, whether in enterprise security operations, academic research, or policy development.

This work is intended for a diverse audience. Cybersecurity professionals will find detailed discussions on defense architecture, governance, and operational resilience. AI users and cloud technology professionals will gain insight into securing the systems they build and manage. Business leaders will benefit from understanding cybersecurity as a strategic function that supports long term growth and trust. Graduate students and researchers will find structured analysis, literature grounded arguments, and references that support further study.

It is important to note that cybersecurity is not a static discipline. Threats evolve, technologies mature, and regulations change. For this reason, the goal of this book is not to offer fixed answers, but to provide a framework for thinking about security in adaptive and sustainable ways. The principles explored here are meant to support continuous improvement rather than one time solutions.

The contributions presented in this book are also part of a broader body of research. In addition to this publication, related peer reviewed journal articles expand on specific aspects of AI, automation, and cloud security management. Together, these works aim to contribute meaningfully to the global conversation on how digital systems can be protected responsibly and effectively.

Ultimately, safeguarding the digital frontier requires more than tools or policies. It requires understanding, collaboration, and a commitment to building systems that are secure by design and resilient by intent. This book is offered as a resource for those who carry that responsibility, and as an invitation to engage thoughtfully with the future of AI and cloud security defense.

FOREWORD

The digital era has ushered in a level of connectivity, automation, and data reliance that was unimaginable only a decade ago. Artificial intelligence now informs how decisions are made, how risks are evaluated, and how systems respond to change. Cloud computing, on the other hand, has become the backbone of modern infrastructure, enabling organizations to operate across borders, scale rapidly, and deliver services with unprecedented efficiency. While these technologies have transformed productivity and innovation, they have also reshaped the cybersecurity landscape in profound and challenging ways.

Security can no longer be treated as a technical afterthought or a support function that reacts to incidents after damage has occurred. Today, cybersecurity is deeply tied to trust, governance, and organizational survival. AI powered systems and cloud based environments introduce layers of complexity that demand a new level of strategic thinking. Threats are no longer limited to known patterns or isolated vulnerabilities. They are adaptive, persistent, and often designed to exploit the very intelligence and scale that modern systems rely upon.

It is within this context that *Guardians of the Digital Frontier: Advanced Strategies in AI and Cloud Security Defense* makes a timely and important contribution. This book does not approach cybersecurity as a narrow technical discipline. Instead, it presents security as an evolving ecosystem that spans architecture, governance, compliance, and leadership. The work recognizes that protecting digital systems requires more than tools. It requires frameworks that can adapt, policies that can endure change, and professionals who understand both the technology and its broader implications.

Oyindamola Oluyemo brings a research driven and structured perspective to this complex field. The depth of analysis throughout this work reflects careful engagement with peer reviewed literature, international security standards, and practical implementation models. The discussion of AI driven defense mechanisms is balanced by a clear recognition of their limitations and responsibilities. This balance is critical in a field where technological optimism can sometimes outpace risk awareness.

One of the defining strengths of this book is its treatment of cybersecurity governance. Many organizations struggle to align innovation with compliance, often viewing regulatory requirements as barriers rather than enablers. This work challenges that mindset by demonstrating how structured governance frameworks can support both security and operational growth. By integrating standards such as ISO 27001 and NIST into adaptive security models, the book shows how compliance can become a continuous and value driven process rather than a periodic obligation.

The exploration of cloud security architecture is equally substantive. As systems become more distributed, the consequences of poor design choices become more severe. This book emphasizes the importance of intentional architecture, resilience planning, and data protection as foundational elements of secure cloud environments. These discussions are particularly relevant for organizations undergoing digital transformation while managing legacy systems and complex operational demands.

The book also speaks directly to the future of cybersecurity. Artificial intelligence introduces new forms of risk, including model manipulation, automation misuse, and governance challenges that are still being defined. By addressing these issues alongside current defense strategies, this work encourages readers to think beyond immediate threats and consider how security practices must evolve over time. This forward looking perspective is essential for professionals tasked with building systems that will remain secure in uncertain conditions.

The audience for this book is broad, and intentionally so. Cybersecurity practitioners will find structured methodologies that inform real world defense and governance. Cloud and AI professionals will gain insight into securing the platforms and systems they design and manage. Business leaders will better understand cybersecurity as a strategic function tied to trust, resilience, and long term sustainability. Graduate students and researchers will benefit from the analytical depth, clear structure, and extensive references that support advanced study.

As digital systems continue to underpin economic activity, public services, and personal interaction, the responsibility to secure them carries global significance. Failures in cybersecurity no longer affect isolated organizations alone. They ripple across supply chains, economies, and societies. Works such as this play an important role in advancing shared understanding and responsible practice in the protection of digital infrastructure.

This book stands as a thoughtful and rigorous contribution to the ongoing conversation around AI and cloud security. It invites readers to engage critically, to question assumptions, and to approach cybersecurity not as a static goal, but as a continuous discipline shaped by technology, policy, and human judgment. For those committed to safeguarding the digital frontier with clarity and purpose, this work offers both guidance and perspective.

INTRODUCTION

Digital technology has become inseparable from how modern societies function. From financial systems and healthcare delivery to education, commerce, and public infrastructure, digital platforms now form the backbone of daily operations across the world. Artificial intelligence and cloud computing sit at the center of this transformation. AI enables systems to learn, predict, and automate decisions at scale, while cloud computing provides the flexible infrastructure required to store data, deploy applications, and connect users globally. Together, these technologies have reshaped productivity, efficiency, and innovation. They have also redefined the nature of cybersecurity risk.

As organizations increasingly depend on AI powered and cloud based systems, the consequences of security failure have grown more severe. A single breach can compromise sensitive data, disrupt essential services, or undermine public trust. Cyber threats are no longer limited to isolated attacks or opportunistic actors. They are persistent, coordinated, and often designed to exploit systemic weaknesses in complex digital environments. This reality has shifted cybersecurity from a technical concern to a strategic and organizational imperative.

Traditional security models were developed for environments that were relatively stable and predictable. Systems operated within clearly defined boundaries, and security controls were often deployed at the perimeter. In contrast, modern digital ecosystems are dynamic. Cloud workloads scale up and down automatically. AI models evolve as they process new data. Users access systems from multiple locations and devices. These changes have dissolved clear boundaries and introduced new attack surfaces that demand more adaptive and intelligent security approaches.

Artificial intelligence occupies a unique position within this landscape. It introduces new risks, including model manipulation, data poisoning, and automation misuse. At the same time, it offers powerful capabilities for defense. AI driven systems can analyze vast volumes of data, identify subtle behavioral patterns, and support continuous monitoring in ways that human analysts alone cannot sustain. When designed and governed effectively, AI can strengthen detection, improve response times, and support proactive risk management. However, these benefits are not automatic. Without careful integration and oversight, AI can amplify existing vulnerabilities or introduce new forms of uncertainty.

Cloud computing presents similar challenges and opportunities. Its adoption has enabled organizations to move faster, reduce infrastructure costs, and innovate more freely. Yet the distributed and shared nature of cloud environments complicates security ownership and accountability. Responsibility is often divided between cloud service providers and customers, requiring clear understanding of roles and obligations. Misconfigurations, weak access controls, and inconsistent security practices remain common causes of cloud related incidents. Protecting data integrity and privacy in such environments requires security to be embedded into architecture and operations rather than added as an afterthought.

This book is grounded in the recognition that cybersecurity can no longer be treated as a collection of isolated tools or reactive measures. Instead, it must be understood as an integrated discipline that spans technology, governance, and human decision making. Effective defense in AI and cloud environments depends on how systems are designed, how risks are managed, and how accountability is maintained over time. It also depends on aligning security objectives with organizational goals rather than positioning them in opposition.

Guardians of the Digital Frontier: Advanced Strategies in AI and Cloud Security Defense explores these themes in depth. The work examines how advanced methodologies and defense mechanisms can be applied to safeguard intelligent and cloud based systems against evolving threats. It brings together concepts from cybersecurity engineering, artificial intelligence, cloud architecture, and governance to present a holistic view of modern digital defense.

A central focus of this book is the integration of artificial intelligence into security frameworks. AI is examined not as a replacement for existing controls, but as an enhancement that can support continuous visibility, adaptive response, and informed decision making. The discussion emphasizes the importance of transparency, accountability, and ethical consideration in AI driven security systems. By grounding these approaches in peer reviewed research and established standards, the book seeks to balance innovation with responsibility.

Equally important is the exploration of secure cloud architecture. The book addresses how cloud systems can be designed to support resilience, data protection, and operational continuity. Topics such as identity and access management, encryption, workload isolation, and recovery planning are examined within the broader context of dynamic and distributed environments. Rather than focusing solely on specific technologies, the discussion highlights principles and patterns that remain relevant as platforms evolve.

Governance, risk management, and compliance form another major pillar of this work. Regulatory requirements such as ISO 27001 and NIST frameworks are increasingly central to how organizations demonstrate accountability and manage risk. Yet compliance efforts often struggle to keep pace with rapid technological change. This book examines how intelligent security frameworks can support continuous compliance by embedding controls into daily operations. In doing so, governance becomes an ongoing process that reinforces security rather than a periodic exercise driven by audits.

The structure of the book reflects its goal of guiding readers from foundational understanding to advanced application. Early chapters establish core cybersecurity concepts and explore the changing threat landscape shaped by AI and cloud adoption. Subsequent chapters focus on practical defense strategies, secure deployment practices, and resilient system design. Later sections address automation, operational scalability, emerging threats, and the role of leadership in sustaining effective security programs. Each chapter builds on the previous one, creating a coherent progression from principle to practice.

This work is intended to serve a diverse audience. Cybersecurity professionals will find structured approaches to defense architecture, governance, and resilience that can inform real world implementation. AI users and cloud technology professionals will gain insight into securing the systems they design and manage, with attention to both technical and organizational considerations. Business leaders will benefit from understanding cybersecurity as a strategic function that supports trust, continuity, and long term value. Graduate students and researchers will find analytical depth, extensive references, and a framework that supports further study and inquiry.

It is important to acknowledge that cybersecurity is not static. Threats evolve, technologies mature, and regulatory expectations change. For this reason, the objective of this book is not to provide fixed solutions, but to offer a way of thinking about security that supports adaptation and continuous improvement. The strategies and frameworks discussed are meant to guide decision making rather than prescribe rigid rules.

The digital frontier will continue to expand as artificial intelligence and cloud technologies become more deeply embedded in everyday life. With that expansion comes responsibility. Securing digital systems is no longer the task of a single team or function. It is a shared obligation that spans developers, security professionals, leaders, and policymakers. This book is offered as a contribution to that collective effort.

By examining advanced strategies in AI and cloud security defense, this work seeks to equip readers with the understanding needed to protect digital assets, preserve trust, and support innovation in an increasingly complex threat landscape. The chapters that follow invite careful engagement with both the challenges and the possibilities of securing the technologies that shape the modern world.

CHAPTER 1

FOUNDATIONS OF THE DIGITAL FRONTIER

Cybersecurity became a defining concern long before artificial intelligence and cloud platforms entered mainstream use. From the earliest days of networked computing, the protection of data, systems, and users has shaped how technology evolves. What has changed is not the existence of cyber risk, but its scale, speed, and sophistication. As digital systems grow more interconnected and intelligent, the foundations of cybersecurity must be clearly understood before advanced defense strategies can be applied.

At its core, cybersecurity is concerned with the protection of information and systems from unauthorized access, disruption, misuse, or destruction. This protection extends across hardware, software, networks, and data, as well as the people and processes that interact with them. In earlier computing environments, systems were often centralized, predictable, and limited in scope. Security controls focused on access restriction, perimeter defense, and basic monitoring. These measures were generally sufficient because systems changed slowly and operated within well-defined boundaries.

The modern digital frontier presents a different reality. Organizations now operate within ecosystems rather than isolated systems. Data moves continuously across platforms, locations, and services. Users access systems remotely, often from multiple devices and networks. Applications depend on third party services and shared infrastructure. Artificial intelligence introduces systems that learn, adapt, and act autonomously based on data inputs. These developments have expanded the attack surface and challenged many long standing security assumptions.

Understanding cybersecurity in this context begins with an appreciation of how threats have evolved. Early cyber threats were often opportunistic and unsophisticated. Attackers exploited known vulnerabilities or weak passwords to gain unauthorized access, usually for curiosity or limited financial gain. Over time, cyber threats became more organized and intentional. Criminal groups, hacktivists, and state sponsored actors began targeting specific organizations, industries, and national infrastructure. Today, cyber-attacks are often persistent, multi stage operations designed to evade detection and achieve long term objectives.

This evolution has been driven by several factors. The widespread digitization of business processes has increased the value of data, making it a primary target for attackers. The rise of cloud computing has concentrated large volumes of information within shared environments, increasing potential impact when security fails. Artificial intelligence has enabled automation and scale on both sides of the threat landscape, allowing attackers to probe systems more efficiently while also offering defenders new tools for analysis and response.

At the foundation of cybersecurity are three widely recognized principles: confidentiality, integrity, and availability. Confidentiality refers to protecting information from unauthorized access or disclosure. Integrity focuses on ensuring that data remains accurate, complete, and unaltered except through authorized actions. Availability ensures that systems and data remain accessible to authorized users when needed. These principles remain relevant regardless of technological change, but how they are achieved has become far more complex.

Confidentiality in modern systems involves more than restricting access to files or databases. It requires managing identities across distributed environments, enforcing least privilege access, and protecting data as it moves between systems. Integrity extends beyond preventing data tampering to ensuring that automated processes and intelligent systems behave as intended. Availability must account for resilience against not only technical failures, but also deliberate attacks designed to disrupt services.

Risk management forms another critical foundation of cybersecurity. Risk is the potential for loss or harm resulting from a threat exploiting a vulnerability. Effective cybersecurity does not eliminate risk entirely, but seeks to identify, assess, and manage it in a way that aligns with organizational objectives. This process involves understanding what assets most valuable, what threats are most likely, and what vulnerabilities exist within systems and processes.

In traditional environments, risk assessment was often periodic and static. In dynamic digital ecosystems, risk is continuously changing. New services are deployed, configurations are modified, and threat actors adapt their techniques. This has made continuous risk assessment and monitoring an essential component of modern cybersecurity. Artificial intelligence plays an increasingly important role in this area by supporting ongoing analysis of system behavior and risk indicators.

Threat actors themselves are a foundational consideration. Understanding who poses a threat and why helps shape effective defense strategies. Threat actors range from individual attackers seeking personal gain to organized criminal groups pursuing financial profit. There are also insiders who misuse legitimate access, either intentionally or through negligence. In some cases, highly resourced state actors target critical infrastructure, intellectual property, or strategic information. Each category of threat actor brings different capabilities, motivations, and levels of persistence.

Equally important is understanding the concept of the attack surface. The attack surface includes all points where an attacker could attempt to gain access to a system. In modern environments, this surface is extensive. It includes user accounts, application interfaces, network connections, cloud services, data storage, and automated processes. Artificial intelligence systems introduce additional surfaces, such as training data pipelines and model interfaces. Reducing and managing the attack surface is a key objective of cybersecurity architecture.

Human factors also form a critical part of the cybersecurity foundation. Technology alone cannot secure systems if users and administrators lack awareness or discipline. Social engineering attacks exploit human behavior rather than technical vulnerabilities, often with significant success. Phishing, credential theft, and misuse of access privileges remain common entry points for attackers. Effective cybersecurity therefore requires training, clear policies, and a culture of accountability.

Governance provides the structure through which cybersecurity is directed and controlled. Governance defines roles, responsibilities, policies, and decision making authority related to security. Without clear governance, security efforts become fragmented and inconsistent. In complex organizations, governance ensures that security objectives align with business goals and regulatory requirements. It also establishes accountability for managing risk and responding to incidents.

Standards and frameworks play an important role in establishing cybersecurity foundations. International frameworks such as ISO 27001 and guidance from bodies such as NIST provide structured approaches to managing information security. These frameworks do not prescribe specific technologies. Instead, they offer principles, controls, and processes that organizations can adapt to their context. Understanding these standards is essential for building security programs that are both effective and auditable.

As artificial intelligence and cloud computing become central to digital operations, the foundations of cybersecurity must expand to accommodate new realities. AI systems rely heavily on data quality, model integrity, and transparency. Cloud environments require shared responsibility, architectural discipline, and continuous oversight. These factors do not replace traditional security principles, but they demand that those principles be applied in new ways.

By understanding how cybersecurity principles have evolved, how threats operate, and how risk is managed, readers are better prepared to engage with advanced defense strategies. The chapters ahead build on these foundations, exploring how artificial intelligence and cloud security architecture can be integrated to protect digital systems more effectively.

The digital frontier will continue to expand as technology advances. Securing it requires not only new tools, but a clear understanding of the principles that underpin effective defense. Cybersecurity, at its foundation, is about protecting trust in digital systems. That trust begins with sound principles, informed judgment, and a commitment to continuous improvement.

1.1 The Expanding Attack Surface in AI and Cloud Driven Systems

One of the most significant shifts in cybersecurity foundations over the past decade has been the dramatic expansion of the attack surface. In earlier computing environments, the attack surface was relatively limited. Systems were hosted on physical servers, networks were internally managed, and access points were few and clearly defined. Security teams could identify critical assets and enforce controls around a known perimeter. As digital systems evolved, this clarity began to erode.

Cloud computing fundamentally altered how systems are built and accessed. Resources are no longer confined to a single physical location or managed by one organization alone. Applications are composed of multiple services, often distributed across regions and providers. Users interact with systems remotely, and automated processes communicate continuously without human intervention. Each of these elements introduces additional points where failures, misconfigurations, or malicious activity can occur.

Artificial intelligence further compounds this complexity. AI systems rely on data pipelines, training environments, model repositories, and inference interfaces. Each stage introduces potential exposure. Training data can be poisoned or manipulated. Models can be accessed, copied, or influenced through poorly secured interfaces. Outputs can be exploited to infer sensitive information. These risks exist alongside traditional vulnerabilities such as weak authentication, misconfigured storage, and insecure application programming interfaces.

The expansion of the attack surface is not solely a technical issue. It is also organizational. As systems grow more complex, responsibility for security becomes more distributed. Development teams, operations teams, cloud providers, third party vendors, and business units all influence security outcomes. Without clear coordination and shared accountability, gaps emerge that attackers are quick to exploit. Understanding the attack surface therefore requires visibility not only into systems, but also into how decisions are made and responsibilities are assigned.

Managing this expanded surface requires a shift in foundational thinking. Security can no longer rely on perimeter defenses alone. Instead, it must assume that any component can become a point of compromise. This assumption underpins modern approaches such as zero trust architecture, where access is continuously verified and privileges are minimized. It also reinforces the need for continuous monitoring, automated policy enforcement, and disciplined system design.

From a foundational perspective, recognizing the expanded attack surface changes how risk is assessed. Rather than focusing on isolated vulnerabilities, organizations must evaluate how interconnected components interact under both normal and adverse conditions. Small weaknesses that appear insignificant in isolation can combine to create significant exposure. This interconnected risk is a defining characteristic of the digital frontier.

Case Study: Cloud Misconfiguration and Cascading Exposure in a Multi Service Environment

A practical illustration of the expanded attack surface can be seen in a large scale cloud migration undertaken by a regional services organization operating across multiple sectors. The organization adopted a cloud first strategy to improve scalability and reduce infrastructure costs. Over time, dozens of applications were deployed using managed cloud services, shared storage, and automated deployment pipelines.

Individually, each component met basic security requirements. Identity and access controls were implemented, encryption was enabled for sensitive data, and network restrictions were defined. However, the overall environment lacked unified visibility. Different teams managed different services, each with slightly different security assumptions. Documentation was fragmented, and ownership of shared resources was unclear.

An attacker did not exploit a sophisticated vulnerability. Instead, they identified a misconfigured storage service that had broader access permissions than intended. This service contained application logs that included temporary credentials generated for internal communication between services. While the credentials were short lived, they were refreshed automatically and stored repeatedly in the logs.

Using these credentials, the attacker gained access to additional services that trusted the compromised component. From there, they were able to map internal system relationships and identify further weaknesses. Although no sensitive customer data was ultimately exfiltrated, the incident forced a full review of the organization's cloud architecture and resulted in service disruptions during remediation.

The root cause of the incident was not a failure of individual security controls, but a failure to manage the attack surface holistically. Each team had secured its own component, but no one had visibility into how components interacted across the environment. The organization treated security as a series of isolated tasks rather than a system wide discipline.

This case highlights a foundational lesson for modern cybersecurity. In AI and cloud environments, security failures often emerge from interactions rather than isolated flaws. Understanding the attack surface requires continuous assessment of how data, identities, and services connect and evolve over time. It also reinforces the importance of clear governance and architectural discipline, themes that will be explored in greater depth in later chapters.

1.2 Human Judgment and Organizational Culture as Foundational Security Controls

While technology defines much of the modern cybersecurity landscape, human judgment remains one of its most influential elements. Advanced systems can monitor activity, enforce policies, and automate responses, but the effectiveness of these controls is shaped by the people who design, deploy, and operate them. In AI and cloud driven environments, human decisions determine how security principles are interpreted and applied. As a result, organizational culture has become a foundational component of cybersecurity rather than a peripheral concern.

Cybersecurity culture refers to the shared values, assumptions, and behaviors that influence how individuals approach security responsibilities. In organizations with strong security culture, employees understand the importance of protecting data and systems, even when it requires additional effort or slows down processes. In contrast, weak security culture often manifests as shortcuts, policy avoidance, and a tendency to treat security as someone else's responsibility.

The rise of cloud platforms and AI powered tools has intensified the impact of human behavior on security outcomes. Cloud environments enable rapid deployment and configuration changes, often with minimal oversight. AI systems rely on human choices related to data selection, model training, and operational use. A single misjudgment can introduce risk that scales quickly across systems. This makes human awareness and accountability central to cybersecurity foundations.

One common challenge is the separation between technical teams and business decision makers. Security controls may be perceived as obstacles to productivity or innovation rather than essential safeguards. When deadlines or cost pressures dominate decision making, security requirements are often relaxed or deferred. Over time, this creates an environment where vulnerabilities accumulate quietly until they are exploited.

Training and awareness programs are frequently presented as solutions to human related risk, but their effectiveness depends on how they are implemented. One time training sessions or generic policy documents rarely change behavior. Effective security culture requires ongoing engagement, clear communication, and leadership support. Employees must understand not only what policies exist, but why they matter and how their actions contribute to overall system resilience.

Accountability is another critical factor. When roles and responsibilities for security are unclear, gaps emerge. In cloud environments, responsibility is shared across providers, administrators, developers, and users. Without explicit ownership, critical tasks such as access reviews, configuration checks, and incident response planning may be neglected. Clear governance structures help ensure that security decisions are deliberate and traceable.

From a foundational perspective, cybersecurity must be treated as a collective discipline rather than a specialized function isolated within security teams. This does not mean that every employee becomes a security expert. It means that security considerations are integrated into daily workflows and decision making across the organization. When security is embedded into culture, systems are more likely to be configured correctly, monitored consistently, and improved continuously.

Case Study: Insider Error and AI Model Exposure in a Research Environment

An illustration of the impact of human judgment on cybersecurity can be found in a research organization developing AI driven analytics tools for commercial partners. The organization operated a hybrid cloud environment where sensitive datasets were used to train machine learning models. Access controls were defined, and data was encrypted both at rest and during processing. On paper, the security framework appeared sound.

However, pressure to accelerate development timelines led to informal practices that weakened these controls. A senior data scientist, seeking to collaborate more efficiently with external partners, created a shared access environment that bypassed standard approval processes. The intention was not malicious. The decision was framed as a temporary measure to support productivity.

Over time, this shared environment became a default collaboration space. Additional datasets and trained models were added without review. Audit logging was limited, and access permissions were broader than necessary. Eventually, an external collaborator accessed a trained model that contained embedded patterns derived from sensitive data. While the raw data was not directly exposed, the model outputs allowed inference of confidential information.

The incident prompted an internal investigation that revealed no technical breach in the traditional sense. There was no external attack, no exploitation of vulnerabilities, and no system failure. The exposure resulted from a series of human decisions made in an environment where security culture was secondary to speed and convenience.

The organization responded by strengthening governance around AI development workflows. Clear approval processes were introduced, access reviews were enforced, and collaboration tools were redesigned to align with security policies. More importantly, leadership emphasized security as a shared responsibility, reinforcing the idea that productivity and protection are not opposing goals.

This case demonstrates a foundational truth of modern cybersecurity. Even the most advanced systems are shaped by human behavior. AI and cloud technologies amplify both good and bad decisions. When security culture is weak, risk accumulates silently. When it is strong, systems are more resilient even in the face of inevitable mistakes.

As organizations continue to adopt intelligent and distributed technologies, recognizing the role of human judgment becomes essential. Cybersecurity foundations are not built solely on architecture and tools, but on how people think, decide, and act within digital environments.

CHAPTER 2

THE RISE OF ARTIFICIAL INTELLIGENCE IN CYBERSECURITY DEFENSE

Cybersecurity entered a new phase when the volume, speed, and complexity of digital activity began to exceed what human driven analysis could reasonably manage. Security teams were suddenly expected to monitor thousands of systems, millions of events, and constantly shifting attack patterns, all while responding in near real time. This pressure exposed a fundamental limitation of traditional security models. Human attention and static rules could no longer keep pace with modern threat environments. It was within this gap that artificial intelligence emerged as a practical and necessary component of cybersecurity defense.

Artificial intelligence in cybersecurity refers to the use of machine learning, data analytics, and automated decision systems to support the detection, analysis, and mitigation of cyber threats. Unlike conventional security tools that rely on predefined signatures or manually configured rules, AI driven systems learn from data. They identify patterns, adapt to change, and improve performance over time. This capability has transformed how security operations are conducted and how risk is understood.

The rise of AI in cybersecurity did not occur in isolation. It was driven by structural changes in digital systems. Cloud computing expanded the scale of infrastructure. Remote work increased the diversity of access points. Application development accelerated through automation and continuous deployment. At the same time, attackers became more sophisticated, using automation, social engineering, and targeted techniques to bypass traditional defenses. These conditions created an environment where intelligence and adaptability became essential.

Early applications of artificial intelligence in security focused on narrow tasks. Spam filtering, malware classification, and basic anomaly detection were among the first areas where machine learning demonstrated value. These systems analyzed historical data to identify known patterns associated with malicious activity. While effective within defined boundaries, they were limited by the quality and scope of the data they were trained on. As threats evolved, so too did the need for more flexible and context aware systems.

Modern AI driven security systems operate across multiple layers of the digital environment. They analyze network traffic, user behavior, system logs, application activity, and data flows simultaneously. By correlating signals across these domains, AI systems can detect subtle indicators of compromise that would be difficult for human analysts to identify in isolation. This holistic perspective is one of the defining strengths of artificial intelligence in cybersecurity defense.

A key concept underlying AI driven security is behavioral analysis. Rather than focusing solely on what an action is, behavioral models examine how actions occur over time. Users, applications, and systems tend to exhibit consistent patterns during normal operation. When behavior deviates from these patterns in meaningful ways, it can signal potential risk. AI systems excel at learning these baselines and identifying deviations at scale.

This approach is particularly valuable in environments where threats do not rely on known signatures. Advanced attackers often use legitimate credentials, trusted tools, and normal system functions to achieve their objectives. These techniques are designed to blend in with routine activity. Signature based tools struggle in such scenarios because there is no obvious indicator to match. Behavioral models, however, can identify misuse by recognizing actions that are contextually abnormal even if they appear technically valid.

Another area where AI has reshaped cybersecurity is incident response. Traditional response processes are often manual and sequential. Alerts are reviewed, evidence is gathered, and decisions are made based on limited information. This approach is slow and prone to error under pressure. AI driven response systems support faster decision making by prioritizing alerts, suggesting remediation actions, and automating containment where appropriate. This reduces response time and limits the potential impact of attacks.

Artificial intelligence has also improved threat intelligence. By analyzing data from multiple sources, including internal logs, external feeds, and historical incidents, AI systems can identify emerging threat trends and attack techniques. This intelligence supports proactive defense by helping organizations anticipate risks rather than reacting after damage occurs. It also supports more informed strategic planning by highlighting where defenses should be strengthened.

Despite these advantages, the rise of AI in cybersecurity defense has introduced new challenges. Machine learning models depend heavily on data quality. Biased, incomplete, or manipulated data can lead to inaccurate conclusions. Attackers may attempt to poison training data or exploit model behavior to evade detection. These risks highlight the importance of transparency, validation, and continuous oversight in AI driven security systems.

There is also the challenge of explainability. Security decisions often carry significant consequences, including service disruption, access restriction, or regulatory impact. When AI systems make or influence these decisions, organizations must be able to understand and justify their actions. Black box models that cannot be explained undermine trust and complicate accountability. As a result, explainable AI has become an important consideration in cybersecurity applications.

Human expertise remains central to effective AI driven defense. Artificial intelligence enhances security operations, but it does not replace human judgment. Analysts are needed to interpret results, refine models, and make contextual decisions that machines cannot. The most effective security programs treat AI as a partner rather than a substitute, combining automation with professional oversight.

Integration is another critical factor in the success of AI driven cybersecurity. AI tools must operate within existing security architectures and workflows. Poor integration can lead to fragmented visibility, duplicated effort, and missed signals. Successful implementation requires careful alignment between AI capabilities, organizational processes, and technical infrastructure. This alignment ensures that intelligence is translated into meaningful action.

From a governance perspective, the use of artificial intelligence in cybersecurity raises important questions. Who is responsible for decisions made by automated systems. How are errors identified and corrected. How is compliance maintained when controls are adaptive rather than static. Addressing these questions requires clear policies, defined roles, and continuous evaluation. AI driven security must be governed with the same rigor as any other critical system.

The rise of AI in cybersecurity defense also reflects a broader shift in how security is conceptualized. Security is no longer a static state achieved through fixed controls. It is a dynamic process that evolves alongside threats and technologies. Artificial intelligence supports this evolution by enabling systems to learn and adapt. However, adaptability must be guided by principle and oversight to avoid unintended consequences.

As organizations continue to adopt AI driven defense mechanisms, foundational understanding becomes essential. Security professionals must understand not only what these systems do, but how and why they operate. This understanding supports responsible use, effective integration, and informed decision making. It also helps organizations assess where AI adds value and where traditional controls remain necessary.

This chapter has explored the forces that led to the rise of artificial intelligence in cybersecurity defense and the ways in which AI has transformed detection, response, and threat intelligence. It has also highlighted the limitations and responsibilities that accompany these capabilities. The chapters that follow will build on this understanding by examining how AI driven defense can be applied within cloud environments, secure architectures, and governance frameworks.

Artificial intelligence is not a cure for all cybersecurity challenges. It is a powerful tool whose effectiveness depends on how it is designed, deployed, and governed. When integrated thoughtfully, AI strengthens the ability to defend complex digital systems. When applied carelessly, it can introduce new risks. Navigating this balance is one of the defining challenges of modern cybersecurity defense and a central theme of this work.

2.1 AI Driven Security Decision Making and the Shift from Reactive to Predictive Defense

One of the most significant changes introduced by artificial intelligence in cybersecurity is the transformation of how security decisions are made. Traditional security operations are largely reactive. Actions are taken after suspicious activity has been detected, alerts have been generated, and potential damage has already begun to unfold. While this model has been effective in controlled environments, it struggles in modern digital systems where threats operate quietly and evolve over time.

Artificial intelligence enables a shift toward predictive defense by focusing on patterns rather than isolated events. Instead of asking whether a specific action violates a predefined rule, AI systems evaluate how activities relate to historical behavior, contextual factors, and evolving risk conditions. This allows security teams to identify situations that are likely to develop into incidents even when no explicit policy violation has occurred.

Predictive defense relies on continuous learning. AI models ingest large volumes of operational data, including user behavior, system interactions, configuration changes, and access patterns. Over time, these models develop an understanding of normal system behavior and recognize deviations that suggest elevated risk. This capability is particularly valuable in complex environments where legitimate activity can closely resemble malicious behavior.

The shift from reaction to prediction changes the role of security teams. Instead of spending the majority of their time responding to alerts, teams can focus on managing risk proactively. This includes investigating emerging risk indicators, strengthening controls before exploitation occurs, and supporting informed decision making across the organization. As a result, security becomes a forward looking function rather than a crisis response mechanism.

Artificial intelligence also improves decision prioritization. Modern security environments generate more signals than human analysts can reasonably assess. AI driven systems evaluate the potential impact and likelihood of different risk scenarios, allowing teams to concentrate on issues that pose the greatest threat to critical assets. This prioritization reduces noise, improves efficiency, and supports more consistent decision outcomes.

However, predictive decision making introduces new responsibilities. Predictions are not certainties. They represent probabilistic assessments that must be interpreted carefully. Overreliance on automated predictions can lead to unnecessary restrictions or missed opportunities. Underuse can result in ignored warnings. Effective implementation therefore requires clear thresholds, validation processes, and regular review of model performance.

Human oversight remains essential. Artificial intelligence can identify trends and suggest actions, but humans provide contextual understanding and ethical judgment. Business priorities, regulatory considerations, and operational constraints must be factored into security decisions. The most effective security programs integrate AI driven insights into structured decision workflows rather than treating them as autonomous commands.

From a governance perspective, predictive defense challenges traditional control models. Many compliance frameworks are based on static controls and documented procedures. Predictive systems are adaptive by nature, which can create tension with audit expectations. Addressing this requires transparent documentation of model behavior, clear accountability for decisions, and alignment between security innovation and governance requirements.

The shift toward predictive defense also influences organizational culture. When security teams are empowered to anticipate risk rather than respond to incidents, collaboration with other departments improves. Security becomes part of planning discussions rather than an obstacle encountered after problems arise. This cultural shift supports more resilient systems and more informed technology adoption.

As artificial intelligence continues to mature, predictive security decision making will become increasingly central to cybersecurity defense. Its effectiveness will depend not only on technical sophistication, but on thoughtful integration, human oversight, and disciplined governance. By embracing prediction as a complement to traditional controls, organizations can better navigate the complexity of modern threat environments.

2.2 Limitations, Risks, and Ethical Boundaries of AI in Cybersecurity Defense

While artificial intelligence has introduced powerful capabilities into cybersecurity defense, it is not without limitations or risk. Understanding these constraints is essential to building realistic expectations and responsible security programs. AI driven systems can enhance detection, analysis, and decision support, but they also introduce new forms of dependency, complexity, and exposure that must be managed deliberately.

One of the most fundamental limitations of artificial intelligence in cybersecurity lies in its dependence on data. Machine learning models learn patterns from historical and real time information. If the data used for training or operation is incomplete, biased, or inaccurate, the resulting insights will reflect those weaknesses. In cybersecurity, this can lead to blind spots where certain attack techniques go undetected or where benign behavior is mistakenly flagged as malicious.

Attackers are increasingly aware of this dependency and may attempt to exploit it. Techniques such as data poisoning involve deliberately introducing misleading data into training sets or operational inputs to distort model behavior. Over time, this can reduce detection accuracy or create predictable weaknesses that attackers can exploit. These risks highlight the importance of data validation, controlled training environments, and continuous model evaluation.

Another challenge is model generalization. AI systems trained in one environment may not perform reliably when conditions change. Cloud configurations, user behavior, and application usage patterns evolve constantly. Without regular retraining and contextual adjustment, models may become outdated and less effective. This issue is particularly relevant in dynamic environments where infrastructure and workflows change frequently.

Explainability presents an additional concern. Many advanced AI models operate as complex statistical systems whose internal reasoning is difficult to interpret. In cybersecurity, where decisions can affect system availability, user access, and regulatory compliance, opaque decision making can undermine trust. Security teams and auditors must be able to understand why certain actions were flagged or taken. Without explainability, accountability becomes difficult to establish.

Ethical considerations further complicate the use of AI in cybersecurity defense. Automated monitoring systems often analyze user behavior in detail, raising concerns about privacy and proportionality. There is a fine line between legitimate security oversight and intrusive surveillance. Organizations must ensure that AI driven security measures respect legal and ethical boundaries, particularly in environments subject to strict data protection regulations.

Bias is another ethical risk. AI systems can inadvertently reinforce existing biases present in training data. In security contexts, this may lead to disproportionate scrutiny of certain users, regions, or behaviors without objective justification. Addressing this risk requires careful data selection, regular bias assessment, and inclusive design practices that account for diverse usage patterns.

Over automation also poses a strategic risk. While automation improves efficiency, excessive reliance on automated responses can reduce human situational awareness. Security teams may become disengaged from decision making processes, increasing the likelihood that subtle or novel threats go unnoticed. Maintaining a balance between automation and human oversight is therefore essential to long term effectiveness.

From a governance standpoint, the use of AI in cybersecurity raises questions about responsibility and control. When an AI system influences or executes security actions, organizations must clearly define who is accountable for outcomes. This includes responsibility for errors, unintended consequences, and compliance failures. Clear governance structures and documented decision pathways help ensure that accountability is preserved.

There is also the risk of misaligned incentives. Organizations may adopt AI driven security tools to signal technological maturity without fully understanding their limitations. In such cases, AI becomes a marketing feature rather than a carefully managed capability. This can lead to false confidence and underinvestment in foundational security practices such as architecture design, access control, and human training.

Recognizing these limitations does not diminish the value of artificial intelligence in cybersecurity defense. Instead, it strengthens its application. By understanding where AI performs well and where caution is required, organizations can deploy these systems more effectively and responsibly. AI should be viewed as an augmentation of human expertise and structured security practices rather than a replacement.

As cybersecurity continues to evolve, ethical awareness, technical discipline, and governance maturity will determine whether AI driven defense strengthens or weakens overall security posture. Addressing limitations openly and proactively is a foundational step toward building trustworthy and resilient AI enhanced cybersecurity systems.

CHAPTER 3

CLOUD COMPUTING ARCHITECTURE AND SECURITY FUNDAMENTALS

Cloud computing has reshaped how digital systems are designed, deployed, and maintained. What began as an alternative to on premises infrastructure has become the dominant model for delivering applications, storing data, and supporting global operations. Organizations now rely on cloud platforms to scale rapidly, reduce capital expenditure, and accelerate innovation. Yet this transformation has also introduced new security challenges that require a clear understanding of cloud architecture and its fundamental security principles.

At its foundation, cloud computing is built on abstraction and shared resources. Physical infrastructure is virtualized and delivered as services that can be provisioned on demand. This abstraction provides flexibility and efficiency, but it also separates users from the underlying systems that support their workloads. As a result, visibility and control must be achieved through architectural design rather than physical access. Security in the cloud therefore depends heavily on understanding how responsibilities are divided and how controls are implemented across layers.

Cloud services are commonly categorized into three primary models: infrastructure as a service, platform as a service, and software as a service. Each model offers different levels of control and responsibility. In infrastructure as a service, organizations manage operating systems, applications, and data, while the provider secures the physical infrastructure. Platform as a service shifts responsibility for operating systems and runtime environments to the provider, leaving customers responsible for applications and data. Software as a service places most operational responsibility with the provider, with customers focusing on user access and data usage. Understanding these distinctions is essential to implementing effective security controls.

The shared responsibility model is a central concept in cloud security fundamentals. Cloud providers are responsible for securing the underlying infrastructure, including data centers, hardware, and core networking components. Customers are responsible for securing what they deploy and manage within the cloud. Misunderstanding this division has been a leading cause of cloud security incidents. Organizations may assume that providers handle security entirely, leaving gaps in areas such as identity management, configuration, and data protection.

Identity and access management forms the cornerstone of cloud security architecture. In cloud environments, identity replaces the traditional network perimeter as the primary control point. Users, services, and applications authenticate and interact through identity based mechanisms. Strong authentication, role based access control, and least privilege principles are essential to preventing unauthorized access. Poorly managed identities can grant attackers broad access across environments, making identity protection a critical priority.

Configuration management is another foundational element of cloud security. Cloud platforms enable rapid deployment through templates, automation, and self-service tools. While this accelerates development, it also increases the risk of misconfiguration. Insecure storage permissions, overly permissive network rules, and exposed management interfaces are common sources of vulnerability. Secure cloud architecture requires consistent configuration standards, automated checks, and continuous monitoring to ensure compliance.

Network security in cloud environments differs significantly from traditional models. Instead of relying on physical firewalls and segmented networks, cloud security uses virtual networks, security groups, and routing policies. These controls must be designed to restrict traffic appropriately while supporting application functionality. Micro segmentation, which limits communication between workloads to what is strictly necessary, has become an important strategy for reducing lateral movement in the event of compromise.

Data protection is a core objective of cloud security fundamentals. Data stored in cloud environments must be protected throughout its lifecycle, including creation, storage, transmission, and deletion. Encryption is a primary control for protecting data confidentiality, but it must be implemented correctly. Key management, access controls, and encryption policies must be clearly defined and enforced. Without proper governance, encryption alone cannot guarantee data security.

Availability and resilience are equally important aspects of cloud security architecture. Cloud platforms are designed to support high availability through redundancy and geographic distribution. However, achieving resilience requires deliberate design choices. Organizations must architect systems to tolerate failure, including outages, attacks, and misconfigurations. Backup strategies, recovery planning, and regular testing are essential to maintaining service continuity.

Monitoring and logging provide the visibility needed to manage cloud security effectively. Cloud environments generate large volumes of operational data, including access logs, configuration changes, and system events. Collecting and analyzing this data supports threat detection, incident response, and compliance. Without comprehensive logging and monitoring, security teams operate with limited insight into system behavior and risk.

Compliance considerations are deeply intertwined with cloud security fundamentals. Regulatory requirements related to data protection, privacy, and operational integrity apply regardless of where systems are hosted. Cloud environments must be designed to support auditability, policy enforcement, and reporting. This requires integrating security controls into architecture rather than relying on manual processes or post deployment checks.

The role of automation is central to maintaining security at cloud scale. Manual configuration and monitoring are insufficient in environments where systems change frequently. Automation supports consistent enforcement of security policies, rapid detection of misconfigurations, and efficient response to incidents. When combined with governance and oversight, automation enhances both security and operational efficiency.

Understanding cloud computing architecture and its security fundamentals provides the foundation for advanced defense strategies. Without this understanding, organizations risk deploying controls that are ineffective or misaligned with how cloud systems operate. The principles discussed in this chapter establish the groundwork for exploring secure cloud deployment, data protection strategies, and resilient architectures in the chapters that follow.

As cloud adoption continues to grow, security fundamentals remain constant even as technologies evolve. Clear responsibility, disciplined design, and continuous oversight are essential to protecting cloud based systems. Mastery of these fundamentals enables organizations to harness the benefits of cloud computing while managing the risks that accompany it.

3.1 Misconfiguration Risk and the Importance of Architectural Discipline in Cloud Security

One of the most common causes of security failure in cloud environments is misconfiguration. Unlike traditional infrastructure, where system changes are often deliberate and infrequent, cloud platforms enable rapid provisioning and continuous modification of resources. This speed, while beneficial for innovation and scalability, increases the likelihood of configuration errors that can expose systems and data to risk.

Misconfiguration occurs when cloud services are deployed or modified in ways that do not align with security requirements. This may include excessive access permissions, unrestricted network rules, unsecured storage resources, or disabled monitoring controls. These issues are rarely the result of malicious intent. More often, they arise from misunderstanding cloud defaults, inconsistent deployment practices, or pressure to prioritize functionality over security.

Architectural discipline is essential for managing this risk. In secure cloud environments, architecture defines not only how systems function, but how they are protected. Disciplined architecture establishes clear patterns for resource creation, access control, and connectivity. These patterns ensure that security principles such as least privilege, isolation, and accountability are applied consistently across environments.

Standardization plays a central role in architectural discipline. By defining approved configurations and deployment templates, organizations reduce variability and limit the opportunity for error. Standardized architectures also support automation, enabling security policies to be enforced automatically rather than relying on manual intervention. This approach is particularly important in large environments where manual oversight cannot scale effectively.

Another critical aspect of architectural discipline is clarity of responsibility. Cloud environments often involve multiple teams with overlapping roles. Without clear boundaries, critical security decisions may be made inconsistently or without appropriate review. Architectural discipline defines who is responsible for configuring resources, approving access, and monitoring changes. This clarity supports accountability and reduces the likelihood of unintended exposure.

Visibility is closely linked to disciplined architecture. Misconfigurations often persist because they are not detected. Secure cloud architectures incorporate monitoring and logging mechanisms that provide continuous insight into system state and configuration changes. When visibility is built into the architecture, security teams can identify deviations quickly and respond before issues escalate.

From a foundational perspective, misconfiguration is not a failure of cloud technology, but a failure of process and design. Cloud platforms provide robust security controls, but these controls must be applied intentionally and consistently. Architectural discipline ensures that security is embedded into system design rather than treated as a separate concern addressed after deployment.

As cloud environments continue to evolve, the importance of architectural discipline increases. Systems become more interconnected, deployment cycles accelerate, and the impact of small errors grows. By prioritizing disciplined design, standardization, and continuous oversight, organizations can reduce misconfiguration risk and strengthen the security foundations of their cloud infrastructure.

3.2 Shared Responsibility and Accountability in Cloud Security Architecture

A defining characteristic of cloud computing is the shared responsibility model. This model outlines how security responsibilities are divided between cloud service providers and customers. While widely referenced, it is often poorly understood in practice. Misinterpretation of shared responsibility has been a consistent contributor to cloud security failures, making it a critical concept within cloud security fundamentals.

Under the shared responsibility model, cloud providers are responsible for securing the infrastructure that supports cloud services. This includes physical data centers, hardware, foundational networking, and the virtualization layers that enable service delivery. Customers, on the other hand, are responsible for securing the workloads, data, identities, and configurations that operate within the cloud. The exact division of responsibility varies depending on the service model, but accountability is never fully transferred.

A common misconception is that moving to the cloud reduces or eliminates the need for internal security controls. In reality, cloud adoption shifts responsibility rather than removing it. Organizations remain accountable for how access is managed, how data is protected, and how applications are configured. When these responsibilities are overlooked, security gaps emerge that attackers can exploit.

Accountability within cloud environments extends beyond technical controls. It also involves governance structures that define who owns security decisions and how those decisions are reviewed. In complex organizations, multiple teams may interact with cloud resources, including development, operations, security, and third party vendors. Without clear accountability, security tasks may be duplicated, ignored, or inconsistently applied.

Effective cloud security architecture incorporates shared responsibility into design and operations. This includes documenting responsibilities clearly, aligning internal policies with provider guidance, and ensuring that teams understand their roles. Architectural decisions should reflect these responsibilities, embedding controls where customer accountability applies and leveraging provider managed protections where appropriate.

Identity management is a key area where shared responsibility is often misunderstood. While cloud providers offer robust identity and access management services, customers are responsible for defining roles, assigning permissions, and enforcing access policies. Weak identity governance can undermine even the most secure underlying infrastructure. Clear accountability for identity management is therefore essential to cloud security.

Another area of shared responsibility involves monitoring and incident response. Providers may offer logging and monitoring capabilities, but customers must enable, configure, and act on them. Incident detection and response typically require collaboration between provider and customer, particularly when incidents involve underlying infrastructure or shared services.

Preparing for this collaboration in advance improves response effectiveness and reduces confusion during incidents.

Shared responsibility also has implications for compliance. Regulatory requirements apply to organizations regardless of where systems are hosted. Cloud providers may support compliance through certified infrastructure and documented controls, but customers are responsible for demonstrating how their use of cloud services meets regulatory obligations. This requires careful mapping of controls, evidence collection, and continuous oversight.

From a foundational perspective, shared responsibility reinforces the importance of intentional cloud security architecture. Security cannot be assumed based on platform choice alone. It must be designed, implemented, and governed with a clear understanding of accountability boundaries. When organizations treat shared responsibility as a collaborative model rather than a transfer of risk, cloud security becomes more effective and resilient.

As cloud adoption continues to expand, clarity around responsibility and accountability will remain essential. Secure cloud architecture depends not only on technical controls, but on shared understanding, disciplined governance, and continuous engagement between providers and customers. Recognizing and operationalizing shared responsibility is therefore a foundational step toward building secure and trustworthy cloud systems.

CHAPTER 4

AI DRIVEN THREAT DETECTION AND RESPONSE SYSTEMS

Cyber threats rarely announce themselves in obvious ways. In modern digital environments, malicious activity is often subtle, gradual, and carefully designed to blend into normal system behavior. Attackers exploit trusted credentials, legitimate tools, and routine processes to avoid triggering traditional security controls. As a result, the effectiveness of cybersecurity increasingly depends on the ability to detect patterns rather than isolated events. This reality has positioned artificial intelligence as a central component of modern threat detection and response systems.

Traditional threat detection relies heavily on predefined rules and known signatures. These approaches are effective for identifying previously observed attacks, but they struggle when threats evolve or when attackers deliberately avoid recognizable patterns. In environments characterized by scale, automation, and constant change, static detection models quickly become outdated. AI driven systems address this limitation by learning from data and adapting to new conditions over time.

AI driven threat detection systems operate by analyzing large volumes of data generated across digital environments. This data may include network traffic, system logs, user activity, application behavior, and configuration changes. Rather than examining each data source in isolation, AI systems correlate signals across multiple domains. This correlation provides context, allowing systems to distinguish between normal variation and meaningful deviation.

A foundational concept in AI driven detection is anomaly identification. Anomalies are activities or patterns that deviate from established norms. In cybersecurity, anomalies do not automatically indicate malicious intent, but they represent situations that warrant closer examination. Machine learning models are well suited to this task because they can learn baseline behavior for users, systems, and applications and update these baselines as conditions evolve.

Behavioral analysis enhances anomaly detection by focusing on sequences and relationships rather than single actions. For example, logging in from a new location may not be suspicious on its own. However, when combined with unusual access timing, privilege escalation, or unexpected data movement, it may indicate compromise. AI systems excel at identifying these compound patterns, which are difficult to capture through simple rules.

Another critical capability of AI driven detection is scalability. Modern organizations generate far more security data than human analysts can process manually. AI systems can operate continuously, analyzing data in real time and highlighting events that require attention. This scalability is essential for maintaining visibility across complex environments without overwhelming security teams.

Threat detection alone is insufficient without effective response. AI driven response systems aim to reduce the time between detection and action. In traditional models, response often depends on manual investigation and decision making, which can delay containment. AI systems support faster response by prioritizing alerts, recommending actions, and in some cases executing predefined responses automatically.

Response automation must be applied carefully. Automated actions such as isolating systems, disabling accounts, or blocking traffic can prevent further damage, but they may also disrupt legitimate operations if applied incorrectly. For this reason, many organizations adopt a tiered approach. Low risk actions may be automated, while high impact decisions require human approval. AI supports this approach by providing context and confidence scores that inform decision making.

AI driven threat response also improves consistency. Human analysts may interpret similar incidents differently depending on experience, workload, or time pressure. AI systems apply the same evaluation criteria across events, reducing variability and supporting standardized response processes. This consistency is particularly valuable in large or distributed security teams.

Integration with security operations is another key factor in effective AI driven detection and response. AI systems must work alongside existing tools such as security information and event management platforms, incident response workflows, and governance processes. Poor integration can result in fragmented visibility and missed opportunities for action. When integration is done well, AI enhances existing capabilities rather than operating as a standalone solution.

Context awareness distinguishes effective AI driven systems from simplistic automation. Context includes asset criticality, user role, business impact, and environmental conditions. An alert involving a development system may warrant a different response than the same activity on a production system handling sensitive data. AI systems incorporate contextual factors to prioritize response and reduce unnecessary disruption.

Learning and adaptation are central to AI driven threat detection. As systems evolve and new threats emerge, models must be updated to remain effective. Continuous learning allows AI systems to incorporate feedback from investigations and incidents. This feedback loop improves accuracy over time and reduces false positives. However, learning must be controlled to prevent drift or exploitation by adversaries.

False positives remain a significant challenge in threat detection. Excessive alerts can overwhelm security teams and lead to alert fatigue, where genuine threats are overlooked. AI systems address this challenge by refining detection models and incorporating contextual information. By reducing noise, AI enables teams to focus on events that truly matter.

Transparency and trust are essential for adoption. Security teams must understand how AI systems reach conclusions and why certain actions are recommended. Without transparency, confidence in automated detection and response is undermined. Explainable AI techniques help bridge this gap by providing insight into model behavior and decision factors.

Governance plays a critical role in AI driven threat detection and response. Organizations must define policies that govern how AI systems are trained, deployed, and monitored. This includes establishing accountability for decisions influenced by AI and ensuring alignment with regulatory requirements. Governance frameworks help ensure that AI enhances security without introducing unmanaged risk.

The use of artificial intelligence in threat detection and response represents a significant evolution in cybersecurity practice. It reflects a shift from static, rule based defense to adaptive, data driven protection. This shift is necessary in environments where threats evolve continuously and operate at scale.

AI driven detection and response systems do not replace foundational security practices. Instead, they build on them. Strong architecture, disciplined configuration, and clear governance remain essential. AI amplifies these foundations by providing intelligence, speed, and scalability.

4.1 Reducing False Positives and Enhancing Signal Accuracy Through AI Driven Correlation

One of the most persistent challenges in cybersecurity operations is the high volume of false positives generated by detection systems. False positives occur when benign activity is incorrectly flagged as malicious. While some level of false alerts is unavoidable, excessive noise can undermine security effectiveness by overwhelming analysts, slowing response, and eroding trust in detection tools. AI driven threat detection systems address this challenge by improving signal accuracy through correlation and contextual understanding.

Traditional detection tools often evaluate events in isolation. A single login attempt, configuration change, or data transfer may trigger an alert based on predefined thresholds. In isolation, these alerts lack sufficient context to determine intent. As a result, security teams spend significant time investigating activities that pose little or no risk. This reactive workload diverts attention from genuine threats and contributes to alert fatigue.

Artificial intelligence improves accuracy by correlating multiple signals across time and systems. Instead of treating each event as independent, AI driven systems examine how events relate to one another. A login attempt may be evaluated alongside access history, device characteristics, network behavior, and subsequent actions. When viewed collectively, these signals provide a clearer picture of whether activity is benign or suspicious.

Contextual correlation also allows AI systems to account for environmental factors. For example, changes associated with routine maintenance, software updates, or business cycles can be recognized as normal patterns rather than threats. Over time, machine learning models refine their understanding of acceptable variation, reducing unnecessary alerts without weakening detection capability.

This refinement process depends on feedback. When analysts investigate alerts and classify outcomes, that information can be used to improve model performance. As models learn from both true positives and false positives, accuracy improves. This continuous learning loop supports long term effectiveness and helps detection systems adapt as environments evolve.

Reducing false positives has strategic implications. When security teams trust their detection systems, response becomes faster and more decisive. Analysts are more likely to act quickly on alerts that are well contextualized and prioritized. This confidence improves operational efficiency and reduces the risk of missed incidents caused by alert overload.

Accuracy also supports better collaboration between security and business teams. Excessive false positives often lead to friction, particularly when automated controls disrupt legitimate activity. By improving signal quality, AI driven systems reduce unnecessary disruption and help align security actions with business needs.

However, reducing false positives must be balanced carefully. Over tuning detection models to minimize alerts can create blind spots. Effective AI driven systems maintain sensitivity to genuine threats while filtering noise. Achieving this balance requires disciplined model management, regular review, and clear performance metrics.

Case Study: Improving Detection Accuracy in a Cloud Based Financial Services Platform

A financial services organization operating a cloud based transaction platform faced persistent challenges related to alert volume. Its security monitoring tools generated thousands of alerts daily, many related to routine customer behavior or automated system processes. Analysts struggled to keep up with investigations, and response times for genuine threats were inconsistent.

To address this issue, the organization implemented an AI driven correlation engine designed to enhance signal accuracy. The system ingested data from network logs, application activity, identity systems, and transaction records. Rather than evaluating alerts individually, the engine assessed how events unfolded across multiple systems and timeframes.

Within the first few months, the system began identifying patterns associated with normal operational behavior, such as batch processing during peak hours and automated account maintenance activities. Alerts generated from these patterns were deprioritized or suppressed. At the same time, the system highlighted combinations of events that historically preceded fraud attempts or account compromise.

One significant outcome involved account access anomalies. Previously, login alerts were triggered whenever users accessed accounts from new locations. Many of these alerts were false positives caused by legitimate travel or mobile usage. The AI system correlated location changes with device history, transaction behavior, and access timing. Alerts were generated only when multiple risk indicators aligned, significantly improving accuracy.

As a result, false positives were reduced substantially, and analyst workload became more manageable. Security teams were able to focus on higher confidence alerts, improving response speed and consistency. Trust in the detection system increased, and collaboration with business units improved due to fewer unnecessary disruptions.

This case illustrates how AI driven correlation enhances threat detection by reducing noise and improving context. By focusing on relationships rather than isolated events, organizations can strengthen security operations while maintaining efficiency. Accurate signals are foundational to effective response, and artificial intelligence provides the scale and intelligence needed to achieve this balance in modern environments.

4.2 Automated Containment and Response Orchestration in AI Driven Security Systems

As cyber threats accelerate in speed and coordination, the window for effective response has narrowed significantly. In many modern attacks, damage occurs within minutes rather than hours or days. This reality has pushed organizations to rethink how response actions are executed once a threat is detected. Artificial intelligence has become central not only to detection, but also to orchestrating timely and proportionate responses that limit impact without destabilizing operations.

Automated containment refers to the ability of security systems to take predefined actions when certain risk conditions are met. These actions may include isolating a compromised workload, suspending user access, restricting network communication, or triggering additional verification processes. AI driven orchestration ensures that these actions are executed consistently and in alignment with contextual risk rather than rigid rules alone.

In traditional environments, response decisions are often delayed by manual investigation and approval processes. While caution is necessary, excessive delay allows attackers to expand their foothold, escalate privileges, and move laterally across systems. AI driven orchestration addresses this challenge by supporting rapid decision pathways that are informed by context, confidence levels, and predefined response policies.

A key advantage of AI driven response orchestration is proportionality. Not every suspicious event warrants aggressive containment. AI systems evaluate risk severity by combining behavioral indicators, asset criticality, and historical patterns. Low confidence events may trigger monitoring or additional logging, while high confidence events may justify immediate isolation. This graduated response reduces unnecessary disruption while preserving security effectiveness.

Response orchestration also improves consistency across environments. In large organizations, different teams may respond differently to similar incidents, leading to uneven outcomes. AI driven systems apply standardized logic to response decisions, ensuring that similar risks are handled in similar ways regardless of time, location, or personnel. This consistency supports both operational stability and audit readiness.

Integration with existing workflows is essential for effective orchestration. Automated responses must align with incident management processes, communication protocols, and governance requirements. AI driven systems often integrate with ticketing platforms, notification tools, and reporting systems to ensure that actions taken by automation are visible and traceable. This transparency supports accountability and post incident analysis.

Despite its benefits, automated response introduces legitimate concerns. Incorrect containment actions can disrupt business operations, impact customer experience, or violate regulatory obligations. For this reason, organizations must define clear boundaries for automation. Human approval may be required for actions with significant impact, while routine or low risk responses can be automated safely. AI supports this balance by providing confidence assessments and decision support rather than acting autonomously without oversight.

Governance remains critical in automated response systems. Policies must define which actions are permitted, under what conditions, and who retains ultimate authority. Continuous testing and review are necessary to ensure that orchestration logic remains aligned with evolving systems and threats. Without disciplined governance, automation can become a source of risk rather than protection.

Case Study: AI Orchestrated Containment in a Distributed Cloud Environment

A technology services organization operating a distributed cloud environment experienced repeated security incidents involving compromised service accounts. These incidents were typically detected after attackers had already accessed internal resources, resulting in time consuming investigations and partial service disruptions. Manual response processes proved too slow to contain activity early.

To address this issue, the organization implemented an AI driven response orchestration framework integrated with its cloud security monitoring systems. The framework was designed to evaluate behavioral risk signals related to service account usage, access timing, and resource interaction patterns. When predefined risk thresholds were exceeded, the system initiated automated containment actions.

In one instance, the AI system detected abnormal behavior associated with a service account that began accessing resources outside its normal scope during unusual hours. The behavior did not violate explicit access policies, but it deviated significantly from historical patterns. Based on the assessed risk level, the system automatically restricted the account's access to sensitive resources and initiated additional authentication checks.

At the same time, the system generated an incident record and notified the security team with a detailed summary of actions taken and the reasoning behind them. Analysts reviewed the incident and confirmed that the account credentials had been compromised through a third party integration. Because containment occurred early, no sensitive data was accessed and service disruption was minimal.

The organization later expanded the orchestration framework to include additional response actions such as temporary network segmentation and workload isolation. Human approval was required for actions affecting customer facing systems, while internal containment actions were automated. Over time, response speed improved significantly, and the average impact of incidents decreased.

This case demonstrates how AI driven response orchestration strengthens cybersecurity defense by reducing response time and enforcing consistent containment strategies. When automation is guided by context, governance, and human oversight, it enhances resilience rather than undermining control. As threats continue to operate at machine speed, the ability to orchestrate timely response becomes a defining capability of modern security systems.

CHAPTER 5

SECURE CLOUD DEPLOYMENT AND DATA PROTECTION STRATEGIES

As organizations deepen their reliance on cloud platforms, the protection of data has emerged as one of the most critical objectives of cybersecurity. Cloud environments host vast volumes of sensitive information, including personal data, financial records, intellectual property, and operational insights. The security of this data depends not only on defensive tools, but on how cloud systems are deployed, configured, and governed from the outset. Secure cloud deployment and data protection therefore form a central pillar of modern cybersecurity strategy.

Secure deployment begins with architectural intent. Cloud environments offer flexibility, but that flexibility must be guided by structure. When systems are deployed without clear security requirements, weaknesses are often introduced during the earliest stages of design. These weaknesses may persist unnoticed as environments scale, increasing the potential impact of future incidents. A secure deployment strategy establishes security expectations before resources are provisioned, ensuring that protection is built into systems rather than retrofitted later.

One of the first considerations in secure cloud deployment is environment segmentation. Separating development, testing, and production environments reduces the risk that vulnerabilities introduced during experimentation will affect live systems. Segmentation also limits access pathways, making it more difficult for attackers to move laterally across environments. Clear separation supports accountability and simplifies monitoring by reducing unnecessary complexity.

Identity and access control play a foundational role in secure deployment. Cloud systems rely heavily on identity based access rather than traditional network boundaries. Users, applications, and automated services interact through assigned identities and permissions. Implementing least privilege access ensures that each identity has only the permissions necessary to perform its function. Excessive permissions increase exposure and magnify the impact of credential compromise.

Access control must be enforced consistently across cloud services. Insecure deployments often result from fragmented identity management, where permissions are defined differently across platforms or teams. Centralized identity governance helps ensure that access policies are applied uniformly and reviewed regularly. This approach reduces the likelihood of orphaned accounts, outdated permissions, and unauthorized access.

Data protection strategies focus on preserving confidentiality, integrity, and availability throughout the data lifecycle. This lifecycle includes data creation, storage, transmission, processing, and deletion. Protecting data at each stage requires a combination of technical controls, operational practices, and governance oversight.

Encryption is a primary mechanism for protecting data confidentiality in cloud environments. Data should be encrypted both at rest and during transmission. However, encryption alone is insufficient without effective key management. Keys must be stored securely, rotated regularly, and accessed only by authorized systems. Poor key management can undermine encryption and expose sensitive information.

Data integrity ensures that information remains accurate and unaltered except through authorized actions. In cloud systems, integrity controls may include checksums, versioning, audit logs, and validation mechanisms. These controls help detect unauthorized changes and support recovery when integrity is compromised. Integrity is particularly important in environments where automated processes rely on data accuracy to make decisions.

Availability is closely tied to deployment strategy. Secure systems must remain accessible to authorized users even during disruptions. Cloud platforms offer redundancy and geographic distribution, but these capabilities must be configured deliberately. Backup strategies, replication, and recovery planning are essential to ensuring that data remains available in the face of outages, attacks, or accidental deletion.

Secure deployment also requires attention to data classification. Not all data carries the same level of sensitivity or risk. Classifying data based on confidentiality and impact allows organizations to apply appropriate protection measures. Highly sensitive data may require additional encryption, restricted access, or isolated storage, while less sensitive data may be protected through standard controls. Data classification supports efficient use of security resources and reduces unnecessary restriction.

Monitoring and auditing are integral to data protection in cloud environments. Continuous monitoring provides visibility into data access, movement, and modification. Audit logs support accountability and enable investigation when incidents occur. Secure deployments ensure that logging is enabled by default and that logs are protected from tampering or unauthorized access.

Compliance considerations further shape data protection strategies. Regulatory requirements related to privacy, data residency, and retention apply regardless of where data is stored. Cloud deployments must support compliance by enabling policy enforcement, evidence collection, and reporting. Designing systems with compliance in mind reduces the burden of audits and minimizes the risk of regulatory violations.

Automation enhances secure deployment by enforcing consistent security controls at scale. Automated templates, policy checks, and deployment pipelines reduce reliance on manual configuration and help prevent errors. When automation is guided by governance, it strengthens security while supporting agility and operational efficiency.

Secure cloud deployment and data protection are ongoing processes rather than one time tasks. As systems evolve and data volumes grow, protection strategies must adapt. Regular reviews, testing, and improvement help ensure that controls remain effective in changing environments.

5.1 Data Lifecycle Governance and Control in Cloud Environments

An often overlooked aspect of cloud security is how data is governed across its entire lifecycle. Many organizations focus heavily on protecting data at rest or during transmission, yet lose visibility once data begins to move across services, regions, and users. In cloud environments, where data is continuously created, transformed, replicated, and archived, effective protection depends on disciplined lifecycle governance rather than isolated controls.

Data lifecycle governance refers to the policies and processes that define how data is handled from creation to deletion. This includes decisions about where data is stored, who can access it, how long it is retained, and how it is securely disposed of when no longer needed. Without clear lifecycle governance, sensitive data can persist indefinitely, accumulate unnecessary exposure, or be accessed in ways that were never intended.

Cloud platforms make data replication and availability easier than ever. While this supports performance and resilience, it also increases the risk of uncontrolled data sprawl. Copies of sensitive data may exist across multiple storage services, backups, and regions, each representing a potential exposure point. Effective lifecycle governance ensures that replication is intentional, documented, and aligned with security requirements.

Retention policies are a critical component of lifecycle governance. Data that is retained longer than necessary increases risk without adding value. Regulatory requirements often specify minimum and maximum retention periods, particularly for personal or financial data. Cloud deployments must enforce retention policies automatically to prevent human error and ensure compliance. Automated expiration and secure deletion mechanisms help reduce exposure and support auditability.

Access control must evolve alongside the data lifecycle. Permissions that are appropriate during data creation or active use may become excessive as data moves into archival stages. Lifecycle aware access control ensures that permissions are reviewed and adjusted as data state changes. This reduces the likelihood that dormant data remains accessible to users or services that no longer require access.

Data movement between cloud services introduces additional governance challenges. Data may flow through analytics platforms, machine learning pipelines, or third party integrations. Each transition creates an opportunity for exposure if controls are not consistently applied. Secure deployment strategies incorporate data flow mapping to identify where data travels and what protections apply at each stage.

Lifecycle governance also supports incident response and investigation. When data handling practices are clearly defined and enforced, security teams can quickly determine what data was affected during an incident and where it resides. This clarity improves response effectiveness and supports regulatory reporting obligations.

From a strategic perspective, lifecycle governance aligns data protection with business objectives. Not all data requires the same level of protection throughout its existence. By defining governance rules based on data sensitivity and usage, organizations can balance security with operational efficiency. This approach avoids excessive restriction while maintaining appropriate safeguards.

Cloud environments provide powerful tools to support lifecycle governance, including policy engines, tagging mechanisms, and automated workflows. However, these tools are only effective when guided by clear governance frameworks. Policies must be defined collaboratively between security, legal, and business stakeholders to ensure that they reflect both risk tolerance and operational needs.

As cloud adoption matures, data lifecycle governance becomes increasingly important. Organizations that fail to manage data beyond initial deployment often face rising security risk, compliance challenges, and operational inefficiencies. By embedding lifecycle governance into cloud deployment and data protection strategies, organizations strengthen their ability to protect sensitive information over time.

This extension of secure cloud deployment emphasizes that data protection is not limited to encryption or access control. It is a continuous process shaped by how data is created, used, and retired. Strong lifecycle governance provides the structure needed to manage this process effectively and prepares organizations for the resilience challenges explored in the next chapter.

5.2 Encryption Strategy and Key Management as Foundations of Cloud Data Security

Encryption is often viewed as the primary safeguard for protecting data in cloud environments. While it is a critical control, its effectiveness depends on how it is implemented, governed, and maintained over time. Encryption without a coherent strategy can create a false sense of security, leaving data exposed through poor key management, inconsistent application, or lack of oversight. A strong encryption strategy therefore forms a foundational element of secure cloud deployment and data protection.

At a basic level, encryption protects data confidentiality by rendering information unreadable to unauthorized parties. In cloud environments, data should be encrypted both at rest and during transmission. Encryption at rest protects stored data from unauthorized access, while encryption in transit protects data as it moves between systems and services. However, encryption alone does not define who can access data or under what conditions. These decisions are governed by key management practices.

Key management determines how encryption keys are generated, stored, rotated, and revoked. Insecure key management undermines even the strongest encryption algorithms. If keys are stored alongside encrypted data, shared too broadly, or left unrotated for extended periods, attackers who gain access to keys can decrypt sensitive information without detection. Effective key management therefore requires separation of duties, strict access controls, and continuous oversight.

Cloud platforms provide managed key management services that simplify many aspects of encryption. These services support centralized control, auditing, and automated rotation. However, relying on managed services does not remove responsibility from the organization. Decisions about who controls keys, how access is granted, and how usage is monitored remain customer responsibilities. Organizations must understand the tradeoffs between provider managed keys and customer managed keys and select approaches that align with risk tolerance and compliance requirements.

Key ownership is an important strategic consideration. In some regulatory contexts, organizations are required to maintain exclusive control over encryption keys. In others, shared responsibility may be acceptable. Cloud security architecture must account for these requirements during deployment rather than attempting to retrofit controls later. Clear policies defining key ownership and access support both security and compliance objectives.

Encryption strategy must also consider performance and usability. Overly complex encryption schemes can introduce latency or operational friction, leading teams to bypass controls. A balanced strategy applies strong protection where it is needed most while supporting efficient system operation. This balance is achieved through data classification, allowing encryption controls to be tailored based on sensitivity and usage.

Visibility and auditing are essential components of effective encryption strategy. Organizations must be able to track when keys are used, by whom, and for what purpose. Audit logs support incident investigation and regulatory reporting. Without visibility into key usage, unauthorized access may go unnoticed. Cloud environments make it possible to centralize key usage monitoring, but this capability must be enabled and integrated into security operations.

Key rotation and lifecycle management further strengthen encryption effectiveness. Regular rotation limits the potential impact of key compromise by reducing the window of exposure. Secure decommissioning ensures that obsolete keys cannot be reused or recovered. These practices require automation to be practical at scale and must be enforced consistently across environments.

Encryption strategy also intersects with data lifecycle governance. As data moves through different stages of use and storage, encryption requirements may change. Archived data may require different controls than active datasets. Lifecycle aware encryption ensures that protections remain appropriate as data state evolves, reducing risk while supporting operational needs.

From a foundational standpoint, encryption and key management represent more than technical controls. They reflect an organization's approach to trust, accountability, and risk management. Well-designed encryption strategies protect sensitive information while enabling secure collaboration and innovation. Poorly designed strategies create hidden vulnerabilities that undermine confidence in cloud security.

As cloud environments continue to expand, encryption strategy and key management will remain central to data protection efforts. Organizations that treat encryption as an integrated component of secure deployment rather than a standalone feature are better positioned to protect sensitive information and meet evolving security expectations.

CHAPTER 6

BUILDING RESILIENT AI AND CLOUD SECURITY ARCHITECTURES

Security in modern digital systems is no longer measured solely by the ability to prevent attacks. Increasingly, it is defined by how well systems continue to operate when failures occur. As artificial intelligence and cloud technologies become deeply embedded in critical operations, resilience has emerged as a core requirement of cybersecurity architecture. Resilient systems are designed not only to resist threats, but to absorb disruption, recover quickly, and adapt to changing conditions without losing integrity or trust.

Resilience begins with an understanding that failure is inevitable. No system, regardless of how well designed, can eliminate all risk. Software bugs, configuration errors, human mistakes, and sophisticated attacks will occur. In AI and cloud environments, these events may unfold rapidly and affect interconnected components at scale. A resilient architecture anticipates this reality and incorporates mechanisms that limit impact and support recovery.

In cloud environments, resilience is closely tied to architectural design. Cloud platforms provide built in capabilities such as redundancy, geographic distribution, and automated scaling. However, these capabilities do not guarantee resilience on their own. They must be used intentionally. Poorly designed systems may still fail catastrophically despite being hosted on robust platforms. Resilience depends on how services are structured, how dependencies are managed, and how failure scenarios are addressed during design.

One foundational principle of resilient architecture is isolation. Systems should be designed so that the failure or compromise of one component does not cascade across the entire environment. In cloud systems, this may involve separating workloads across accounts, projects, or virtual networks. It may also include limiting shared services and restricting communication pathways between components. Isolation reduces blast radius and makes incidents easier to contain.

Redundancy is another key element of resilience. Redundant systems provide alternative pathways for service delivery when primary components fail. In cloud environments, redundancy can be achieved through multiple availability zones, regions, or service instances. However, redundancy must be carefully managed. Redundant components that share the same configuration errors or credentials may fail simultaneously. True resilience requires diversity in design and control.

Artificial intelligence introduces additional considerations for resilience. AI systems rely on data pipelines, model training processes, and inference services that must remain reliable under stress. If data inputs are disrupted or corrupted, AI driven decisions may degrade or become unreliable. Resilient AI architecture therefore includes safeguards such as data validation, model versioning, and fallback mechanisms that allow systems to operate safely when AI outputs are uncertain.

Monitoring and observability play a critical role in resilience. Organizations cannot respond effectively to failures they cannot see. Cloud and AI systems generate vast amounts of operational data that can be used to assess system health. Metrics, logs, and traces provide insight into performance, behavior, and anomalies. Resilient architectures incorporate observability as a design requirement rather than an optional feature.

Automated recovery is another defining characteristic of resilient systems. Manual recovery processes are often too slow and error prone to meet modern availability expectations. Cloud platforms support automation through orchestration tools, infrastructure templates, and policy engines. When integrated properly, these tools enable systems to restart services, reallocate resources, or roll back changes without human intervention. Automation reduces downtime and supports consistent recovery outcomes.

Security resilience also depends on strong identity and access architecture. During incidents, attackers may attempt to exploit recovery processes or elevated privileges. Resilient systems enforce strict access controls even during failure conditions. Emergency access procedures must be clearly defined, monitored, and audited to prevent misuse. Identity resilience ensures that recovery does not introduce new vulnerabilities.

Data resilience is equally important. Protecting data integrity and availability during disruptions requires robust backup and recovery strategies. Backups must be isolated from primary systems to prevent simultaneous compromise. Recovery procedures must be tested regularly to ensure that data can be restored accurately and quickly. In AI driven environments, this includes preserving training data, model artifacts, and configuration states.

Resilience extends beyond technical design to operational practices. Incident response planning, disaster recovery testing, and cross team coordination are essential components of resilient security architecture. Organizations that regularly simulate failure scenarios are better prepared to respond when real incidents occur. These exercises reveal weaknesses in design, communication, and decision making that may not be apparent during normal operations.

Governance also influences resilience. Clear ownership of systems and processes ensures that decisions are made quickly and responsibly during incidents. Ambiguity around authority can delay response and exacerbate impact. Resilient organizations define escalation paths, decision rights, and communication protocols in advance. This clarity supports coordinated action under pressure.

Artificial intelligence can enhance resilience by supporting adaptive response. AI systems can analyze incident data, predict potential impact, and recommend recovery actions. Over time, these insights can inform architectural improvements and operational adjustments. However, reliance on AI during incidents must be balanced with human oversight to ensure that decisions remain aligned with business priorities and ethical considerations.

Resilient security architecture also supports long term sustainability. Systems that fail frequently or require constant manual intervention erode trust and increase operational cost. By designing for resilience, organizations reduce downtime, improve reliability, and support continuous innovation. This stability is particularly important in environments where AI driven decisions affect customers, partners, or public services.

Building resilient AI and cloud security architectures requires a shift in mindset. Security is no longer about creating impenetrable defenses. It is about designing systems that expect stress and respond gracefully. This approach acknowledges uncertainty and focuses on adaptability rather than perfection.

As threat landscapes continue to evolve, resilience will remain a defining measure of cybersecurity maturity. Organizations that invest in resilient architecture are better equipped to manage disruption, protect critical assets, and maintain trust in digital systems.

6.1 Designing for Failure Tolerance and Graceful Degradation

A resilient security architecture does not assume continuous optimal performance. Instead, it is designed with the expectation that components will fail, degrade, or behave unpredictably under stress. Failure tolerance refers to a system's ability to continue functioning despite partial failure, while graceful degradation describes how a system reduces functionality in a controlled manner rather than collapsing entirely. Together, these concepts form a critical foundation for resilience in AI and cloud security architectures.

In traditional systems, failure often resulted in complete service interruption. A single point of failure could bring down entire applications or expose sensitive data. Cloud environments offer opportunities to move beyond this fragility, but only when failure tolerance is intentionally designed into the architecture. This requires identifying critical dependencies and ensuring that no single component can compromise the entire system.

Failure tolerant design begins with dependency awareness. AI driven and cloud based systems rely on interconnected services such as data stores, identity providers, application interfaces, and external integrations. Each dependency introduces risk. When one service becomes unavailable or compromised, its impact should be contained. Mapping dependencies helps architects understand where failure could propagate and where controls are needed to prevent cascading disruption.

Graceful degradation ensures that when systems are under stress, they continue to operate at a reduced but acceptable level. For example, an AI driven recommendation system may temporarily disable advanced features if data inputs become unreliable, while preserving core functionality. In security contexts, graceful degradation may involve limiting access to non-essential services or reducing automation while maintaining critical protections. This approach prioritizes safety and continuity over completeness.

In AI systems, graceful degradation is particularly important because model outputs may become unreliable when inputs are incomplete or corrupted. Resilient architectures include mechanisms to detect uncertainty and adjust behavior accordingly. This may involve reverting to simpler decision rules, increasing human oversight, or pausing automated actions until confidence is restored. Such controls prevent AI systems from amplifying errors during periods of instability.

Cloud platforms support failure tolerance through features such as load balancing, service replication, and health checks. However, these features must be configured thoughtfully. Automated failover without proper validation can redirect traffic to compromised or misconfigured components. Failure tolerance therefore requires not only redundancy, but intelligent validation of system state before recovery actions occur.

Security controls must also support graceful degradation. During incidents, aggressive containment measures may disrupt legitimate operations. Resilient security architectures balance containment with continuity by defining response tiers. Low risk anomalies may trigger monitoring, while higher risk events justify restrictive actions. This tiered approach allows systems to respond proportionately rather than defaulting to extreme measures.

Human processes play a role in graceful degradation as well. During major incidents, decision making may be constrained by incomplete information and time pressure. Clear guidelines for degraded operation help teams act consistently and avoid ad hoc decisions that introduce additional risk. These guidelines should be tested through simulations to ensure they are practical and well understood.

Designing for failure tolerance also improves long term system evolution. When architectures assume imperfection, changes can be introduced with less risk. New services can be deployed alongside existing ones, and components can be retired gradually. This flexibility supports continuous improvement while maintaining security and availability.

From a governance perspective, failure tolerance and graceful degradation must be explicitly recognized as design objectives. Metrics such as uptime alone are insufficient to measure resilience. Organizations must also consider how systems behave under stress and how quickly they recover acceptable levels of service. These considerations inform investment decisions and architectural priorities.

In AI and cloud security architectures, resilience is not achieved by eliminating failure. It is achieved by managing failure intelligently. Systems that tolerate disruption and degrade gracefully preserve trust, reduce impact, and enable recovery. This design philosophy strengthens security foundations and prepares organizations to operate reliably in unpredictable environments.

6.2 Redundancy, Diversity, and Eliminating Single Points of Failure

A core principle of resilient security architecture is the deliberate elimination of single points of failure. In complex AI and cloud environments, failures rarely occur in isolation. They often cascade across tightly coupled components, turning small issues into widespread disruption. Redundancy and diversity are essential strategies for preventing such cascading failures and ensuring that systems remain functional even when individual elements fail.

Redundancy involves providing multiple instances of critical components so that the failure of one does not interrupt service. In cloud environments, redundancy is commonly implemented through replicated services across availability zones or geographic regions. However, redundancy alone does not guarantee resilience. Redundant components that share identical configurations, credentials, or dependencies may fail simultaneously. True resilience requires thoughtful design that considers how redundancy is implemented.

Diversity strengthens redundancy by reducing the likelihood that multiple components will fail for the same reason. Diversity may involve using different software versions, separate configurations, or distinct service pathways. In AI driven systems, diversity can include maintaining multiple models trained on different datasets or using alternative decision pathways when confidence is low.

This approach reduces systemic risk by ensuring that a single flaw does not compromise all components.

Single points of failure often emerge unintentionally through convenience or oversight. Shared identity providers, centralized configuration stores, or common deployment pipelines can become critical dependencies. While centralization simplifies management, it also concentrates risk. Resilient architecture balances central control with distributed execution, ensuring that failure in one area does not incapacitate the entire system.

In cloud security, network design plays a critical role in eliminating single points of failure. Routing dependencies, gateway services, and firewall configurations must be examined carefully. If all traffic depends on a single network component, its failure can disrupt access and monitoring simultaneously. Distributed networking and segmented access pathways help reduce this risk.

Artificial intelligence systems introduce additional considerations. AI driven decision making may rely on centralized inference services or shared data sources. If these components become unavailable or compromised, dependent systems may behave unpredictably. Resilient AI architectures incorporate fallback mechanisms, such as local inference, cached models, or rule based alternatives, to maintain safe operation during disruption.

Operational processes can also create single points of failure. When only one team or individual understands a critical system, response becomes vulnerable to human availability. Resilient organizations document systems thoroughly, cross train personnel, and automate routine tasks to reduce reliance on individual expertise. This operational redundancy supports continuity during incidents and reduces response delays.

Testing is essential to validating redundancy and diversity. Many organizations assume that redundant systems will function as expected without verifying failure scenarios. Regular testing of failover mechanisms, dependency isolation, and recovery processes reveals weaknesses that may not be apparent during normal operations. Testing also reinforces confidence that resilience measures will perform under real conditions.

From a security perspective, redundancy and diversity must be implemented carefully to avoid increasing attack surface. Additional components introduce new access points and configuration requirements. Resilient architecture ensures that redundant systems are protected with the same rigor as primary components. Governance and automation help maintain consistent security controls across all instances.

Redundancy and diversity support resilience not by preventing failure, but by limiting its impact. When systems are designed to continue operating despite component failure, disruptions become manageable rather than catastrophic. This approach aligns with the broader goal of resilient security architecture, which is to preserve essential functions and protect trust even under adverse conditions.

As AI and cloud environments grow more complex, eliminating single points of failure becomes increasingly challenging and increasingly important. Redundancy and diversity provide practical strategies for managing this complexity. When applied deliberately, they form a strong foundation for resilient systems that can withstand both technical failure and malicious attack.

6.3 Continuous Testing, Simulation, and Adaptive Improvement for Long Term Resilience

Resilience in AI and cloud security architectures cannot be achieved through design alone. Even the most carefully planned systems will degrade over time as technologies evolve, usage patterns change, and threat actors adapt. Continuous testing and simulation are therefore essential to sustaining resilience beyond initial deployment. These practices ensure that assumptions about system behavior remain valid and that weaknesses are identified before they result in failure.

Testing for resilience differs from traditional functional testing. Rather than verifying whether systems perform as intended under normal conditions, resilience testing examines how systems behave under stress, failure, and uncertainty. This includes testing how components respond to service outages, network latency, data corruption, and unexpected load. In security contexts, testing also explores how systems respond to attack scenarios and operational errors.

Simulation provides a controlled environment for exploring failure scenarios without risking production systems. By simulating incidents such as credential compromise, service disruption, or data unavailability, organizations can observe system behavior and response effectiveness. These simulations reveal dependencies and interactions that may not be apparent through documentation alone. Over time, they help teams understand where resilience measures succeed and where improvement is needed.

AI driven systems benefit particularly from continuous testing. Machine learning models may perform well initially but degrade as data distributions change. This phenomenon, often referred to as model drift, can reduce detection accuracy or lead to unintended behavior. Regular testing of model performance under varied conditions helps identify drift early and supports timely retraining or adjustment.

Adaptive improvement is the process of using insights gained from testing and simulation to strengthen architecture and operations. Resilient organizations treat incidents and near misses as learning opportunities rather than isolated failures. Post incident reviews, testing results, and operational metrics inform architectural refinements, policy updates, and training initiatives. This feedback loop supports continuous improvement and reduces the likelihood of repeated failure.

Automation enhances the effectiveness of continuous testing. Cloud platforms support automated testing frameworks that can regularly validate configurations, access controls, and recovery processes. Automated security testing reduces reliance on manual effort and ensures that tests are conducted consistently. When combined with monitoring, automation enables rapid identification of deviations from expected behavior.

Organizational culture plays a critical role in supporting continuous testing. Teams must be encouraged to explore failure scenarios without fear of blame. A culture that values learning and transparency enables honest assessment of weaknesses and fosters collaboration across disciplines. Leadership support is essential to ensuring that resilience testing is prioritized alongside feature development and operational objectives.

Governance frameworks should incorporate resilience testing as a formal requirement. Clear expectations regarding test frequency, scope, and reporting ensure that testing is not treated as optional. Metrics related to recovery time, service degradation, and response effectiveness provide measurable indicators of resilience maturity. These metrics support informed decision making and investment planning.

Continuous testing also supports compliance and audit readiness. Many regulatory frameworks require evidence of risk management and control effectiveness. Documented testing and simulation activities demonstrate due diligence and proactive risk management. This documentation can be invaluable during audits or investigations following incidents.

As AI and cloud technologies continue to evolve, resilience will remain a moving target. Continuous testing and adaptive improvement ensure that security architecture evolves alongside these changes. Rather than relying on static designs, resilient organizations embrace iteration and learning as core practices.

CHAPTER 7

GOVERNANCE, RISK MANAGEMENT, AND COMPLIANCE IN AI AND CLOUD SECURITY

Cybersecurity does not operate in isolation from organizational decision making. As artificial intelligence and cloud technologies become integral to business operations, security must be guided by structured governance, informed risk management, and consistent compliance practices. Without these foundations, even well designed technical controls can fail due to misalignment, oversight gaps, or unclear accountability. Governance, risk management, and compliance provide the framework through which security objectives are defined, enforced, and evaluated.

Governance establishes how security decisions are made and who is responsible for them. In AI and cloud environments, governance defines the policies, roles, and processes that guide the use of technology. Effective governance ensures that security priorities align with organizational goals and that tradeoffs between innovation, cost, and protection are made deliberately rather than by default. Without governance, security efforts become fragmented and reactive.

Clear role definition is a cornerstone of effective governance. Cloud and AI systems often involve multiple stakeholders, including technical teams, business leaders, legal advisors, and external partners. Governance structures clarify who owns data, who approves access, and who is accountable for managing risk. This clarity supports faster decision making and reduces the likelihood of gaps or duplication.

Risk management translates governance objectives into actionable priorities. Risk in cybersecurity refers to the potential impact of threats exploiting vulnerabilities. In AI and cloud environments, risk is dynamic and influenced by rapid change. Effective risk management requires continuous assessment rather than periodic review. Organizations must identify critical assets, evaluate threat likelihood, and assess potential impact in light of evolving conditions.

Risk assessment in AI driven systems introduces unique considerations. Automated decision making can amplify both positive and negative outcomes. Errors or bias in AI systems may affect large populations quickly. Risk management must therefore consider not only technical vulnerabilities, but also model behavior, data quality, and ethical implications. This broader view supports more informed security planning.

Cloud environments also influence risk management practices. Shared infrastructure, distributed services, and third party dependencies introduce risks that extend beyond organizational boundaries. Risk assessments must account for provider responsibilities, contractual obligations, and supply chain exposure. This requires close collaboration between security, procurement, and legal teams.

Compliance provides a structured way to demonstrate that security practices meet regulatory and contractual requirements. Regulations related to data protection, privacy, and operational integrity apply regardless of deployment model. In AI and cloud contexts, compliance requires careful mapping of controls to regulatory expectations. Cloud providers may support compliance through certified infrastructure, but organizations remain responsible for how services are used.

One challenge in compliance is maintaining evidence of control effectiveness. AI driven systems and automated deployments change frequently, making static documentation insufficient. Compliance programs must evolve to capture dynamic evidence such as logs, configuration states, and access records. Automation can support this by collecting and organizing evidence continuously.

Governance, risk management, and compliance are interconnected. Governance defines objectives and accountability. Risk management identifies priorities and tradeoffs. Compliance validates that controls are implemented and maintained. When these functions operate in isolation, security efforts become inefficient and inconsistent. Integrated frameworks support coherence and resilience.

Organizational culture plays a significant role in the effectiveness of governance and risk management. Policies and controls are only as effective as the behaviors they influence. Leadership commitment to security sets expectations and shapes decision making. When governance is perceived as a constraint rather than an enabler, compliance becomes superficial and risk increases.

Artificial intelligence can support governance and risk management by providing insights into system behavior and emerging risks. Analytics can highlight trends, identify policy violations, and support informed decision making. However, reliance on AI for governance must be balanced with human oversight to ensure accountability and ethical judgment.

As regulatory landscapes continue to evolve, particularly around data protection and AI use, governance frameworks must remain adaptable. Static policies quickly become outdated. Effective governance includes mechanisms for review and revision, ensuring that security practices evolve alongside technology and regulation.

7.1 Establishing Accountability and Decision Ownership in AI and Cloud Governance

One of the most persistent weaknesses in cybersecurity governance is the absence of clear accountability. In AI and cloud environments, systems are often built and managed by multiple teams using shared platforms and automated processes. While this collaborative model enables speed and innovation, it can obscure responsibility when security decisions must be made or when failures occur. Establishing accountability and decision ownership is therefore a critical element of effective governance.

Accountability in cybersecurity governance refers to the clear assignment of responsibility for decisions, actions, and outcomes related to security. This includes ownership of data, control of access, approval of system changes, and response to incidents. In the absence of defined ownership, security risks may be ignored or deferred because no individual or team feels empowered or obligated to address them.

AI driven systems add complexity to accountability structures. Decisions may be influenced by automated models that operate across departments and functions. When outcomes are undesirable, it can be difficult to determine whether responsibility lies with developers, data owners, system operators, or governance bodies. Effective governance anticipates this challenge by defining accountability at each stage of system design and operation.

Decision ownership is closely linked to accountability. Governance frameworks must specify who has the authority to make security related decisions and under what conditions. This includes decisions about deploying new AI models, approving cloud configurations, granting elevated access, and responding to detected risks. Clear decision ownership reduces delays and prevents inconsistent responses during critical moments.

Cloud environments further complicate accountability due to shared responsibility with service providers. While providers manage underlying infrastructure, customers remain accountable for how services are configured and used. Governance frameworks must reflect this division clearly. Contracts and internal policies should align to ensure that responsibilities are understood and enforced across organizational boundaries.

Effective accountability structures also support transparency. When decisions are documented and ownership is clear, organizations can review actions taken during incidents or audits. This transparency supports learning and continuous improvement. It also strengthens trust with regulators, partners, and customers by demonstrating disciplined management of security risk.

Organizational design plays an important role in establishing accountability. Security governance should not be confined to technical teams alone. Business leaders, legal advisors, and risk managers must be involved in defining acceptable risk and approving tradeoffs. This shared governance approach ensures that security decisions reflect organizational priorities rather than isolated technical considerations.

Case Study: Governance Breakdown in an AI Enabled Cloud Deployment

A large enterprise deployed an AI driven analytics platform in a cloud environment to support strategic decision making across multiple business units. The platform processed sensitive operational data and relied on automated models to generate insights. Development, deployment, and operation of the platform were distributed across several teams, each with distinct responsibilities.

Over time, changes were made to data ingestion processes and model parameters to support new use cases. These changes were implemented quickly to meet business demand, but governance oversight was limited. No single team was clearly accountable for approving changes that affected data sensitivity and access controls. Documentation was fragmented, and decision ownership was unclear.

A routine internal review later revealed that sensitive datasets had been made accessible to additional users through automated workflows that bypassed established approval processes. While no external breach occurred, the exposure represented a significant governance failure. The organization struggled to determine who had authorized the changes and why risk assessments were not conducted.

The incident prompted a comprehensive review of governance structures. The organization introduced clear accountability for AI and cloud systems by assigning data ownership, model ownership, and platform ownership roles. Decision rights were documented, and approval workflows were enforced through automated controls. Changes affecting sensitive data or model behavior required review by a cross functional governance committee.

Following these changes, visibility into system modifications improved significantly. Security reviews became more consistent, and teams gained clarity around their responsibilities. The organization also improved audit readiness by maintaining clear records of decisions and approvals related to AI and cloud deployments.

7.2 Managing Regulatory Alignment and Cross Border Compliance in Cloud and AI Systems

As organizations expand their use of cloud platforms and artificial intelligence, regulatory compliance has become increasingly complex. Data often flows across geographic boundaries, cloud services operate in multiple jurisdictions, and AI systems process information subject to diverse legal and ethical standards. Managing regulatory alignment in this context requires more than awareness of individual regulations. It demands structured governance that accounts for variation, overlap, and change across regulatory environments.

Regulatory requirements related to data protection, privacy, and security differ significantly by region. Laws governing personal data, financial information, and critical infrastructure impose specific obligations on how data is collected, stored, processed, and shared. In cloud and AI environments, these obligations apply regardless of where systems are hosted or how data is processed. Organizations remain responsible for ensuring compliance even when services are delivered through third party platforms.

Cross border data movement is a central challenge. Cloud architectures often distribute data across regions to support performance and resilience. AI systems may aggregate data from multiple sources to improve accuracy. Without careful governance, these practices can conflict with data residency or sovereignty requirements. Effective compliance management requires visibility into where data resides and how it moves across systems.

AI systems introduce additional regulatory considerations. Automated decision making may be subject to transparency, fairness, and accountability requirements. In some jurisdictions, individuals have rights related to how automated decisions affect them. Compliance frameworks must therefore address not only technical security controls, but also how AI models are trained, validated, and deployed.

Governance structures play a critical role in managing regulatory alignment. Policies must define how regulatory requirements are interpreted and implemented across systems. This includes establishing acceptable deployment models, defining approval processes for new use cases, and ensuring that compliance considerations are integrated into system design rather than addressed after deployment.

Documentation and evidence collection are essential components of compliance. Regulators and auditors often require proof that controls are implemented and effective. In dynamic cloud and AI environments, static documentation quickly becomes outdated. Automated evidence collection, including configuration records, access logs, and model performance metrics, supports continuous compliance and reduces audit burden.

Collaboration between legal, security, and technical teams is necessary to manage regulatory complexity. Legal teams interpret regulatory obligations, security teams translate these obligations into controls, and technical teams implement them in practice. Without coordination, gaps emerge that expose organizations to regulatory risk.

Case Study: Navigating Multi Jurisdiction Compliance in an AI Enabled Cloud Platform

A global organization operating an AI enabled customer engagement platform faced growing regulatory complexity as it expanded into new markets. The platform processed personal data and used machine learning models to personalize interactions. Data was stored and processed in a distributed cloud environment spanning multiple regions.

Initially, compliance efforts focused on meeting requirements in the organization's primary market. As operations expanded, differences in data protection laws across regions introduced challenges. Some jurisdictions imposed strict data residency requirements, while others emphasized transparency in automated decision making. The organization lacked a unified framework for managing these differences.

During a regulatory inquiry in one region, the organization struggled to demonstrate where specific data sets were stored and how AI decisions were generated. Although no enforcement action was taken, the inquiry highlighted weaknesses in governance and documentation.

In response, the organization implemented a centralized compliance governance framework. Data flows were mapped across regions, and deployment architectures were adjusted to align with residency requirements. AI model documentation was standardized to support transparency and accountability. Automated compliance checks were introduced to monitor configuration drift and policy adherence.

These changes improved the organization's ability to respond to regulatory inquiries and reduced uncertainty around compliance obligations. Teams gained clearer guidance on how to design systems that met diverse regulatory expectations, and governance oversight became more proactive rather than reactive.

CHAPTER 8

IDENTITY ACCESS CONTROL AND SECURE COLLABORATION

Security in modern digital environments is increasingly defined by who can access systems rather than where those systems are located. As cloud platforms dissolve traditional network boundaries and artificial intelligence automates decision making, identity has become the primary control point for protecting digital assets. Identity, access control, and secure collaboration now sit at the core of cybersecurity strategy, shaping how users, applications, and services interact within distributed environments.

In traditional architectures, security relied heavily on perimeter defenses. Firewalls, network segmentation, and physical access controls were used to define trusted and untrusted zones. Cloud computing fundamentally changed this model. Users access systems remotely, services communicate across networks, and applications depend on shared infrastructure. In this context, identity replaces the perimeter as the foundation of trust. Every access request must be evaluated based on identity, context, and intent.

Identity in cloud and AI environments extends beyond human users. Applications, services, and automated processes operate using identities that authenticate and authorize actions. These non-human identities often have broad privileges and operate continuously, making them attractive targets for attackers. Effective identity management must therefore address both human and machine identities with equal rigor.

Access control defines what identities are allowed to do once authenticated. In secure systems, access is granted based on the principle of least privilege. Each identity receives only the permissions necessary to perform its function. Excessive permissions increase exposure and amplify the impact of compromise. In cloud environments, where permissions can span multiple services and resources, disciplined access control is essential.

Role based access control provides a structured way to manage permissions by grouping privileges according to function. Roles simplify administration and reduce the risk of inconsistent permission assignment. However, roles must be designed carefully to avoid becoming overly broad. Regular review of role definitions and assignments helps ensure that access remains aligned with operational needs.

Contextual access control enhances traditional models by considering additional factors such as location, device state, time of access, and behavior. In AI enhanced environments, contextual signals can be evaluated dynamically to adjust access decisions in real time. For example, access may be restricted when unusual behavior is detected or when risk levels increase. This adaptive approach improves security without relying solely on static rules.

Secure collaboration introduces additional complexity. Cloud platforms enable teams to collaborate across organizational and geographic boundaries. Data is shared with partners, contractors, and external services. While collaboration supports productivity, it also expands the attack surface. Secure collaboration requires clear policies governing who can access shared resources and under what conditions.

Identity federation is commonly used to support secure collaboration. Federation allows external users to access resources using their own trusted identity providers. This reduces the need to manage separate credentials and improves user experience. However, federation must be governed carefully. Trust relationships must be clearly defined, and access must be limited to necessary resources only.

Artificial intelligence plays an increasing role in identity and access management. AI systems analyze access patterns to identify anomalies, support adaptive authentication, and detect potential compromise. These capabilities strengthen access control by responding to risk dynamically. However, AI driven access decisions must be transparent and auditable to maintain trust and accountability.

Credential protection remains a critical concern. Phishing, credential reuse, and account compromise continue to be common attack vectors. Strong authentication mechanisms such as multi factor authentication significantly reduce risk. In cloud environments, authentication controls must be enforced consistently across all access points, including administrative interfaces and application programming interfaces.

Lifecycle management is essential to maintaining secure access. Identities must be created, modified, and removed in alignment with changes in role and responsibility. Dormant accounts and outdated permissions create hidden vulnerabilities. Automated lifecycle management ensures that access is updated promptly and reduces reliance on manual processes.

Monitoring and auditing support accountability in identity and access control. Logs of authentication attempts, access requests, and permission changes provide visibility into system usage and support investigation when incidents occur. In secure architectures, monitoring is continuous and integrated into security operations rather than treated as an afterthought.

Secure collaboration also requires cultural alignment. Users must understand their responsibilities when sharing data and accessing systems. Training and awareness programs help reinforce appropriate behavior and reduce the likelihood of accidental exposure. Clear communication about access policies supports compliance and trust.

Governance provides the structure that ensures identity and access controls are applied consistently. Policies define acceptable access practices, approval processes, and enforcement mechanisms. Governance also ensures alignment with regulatory requirements related to data protection and privacy.

Identity, access control, and secure collaboration form the backbone of security in AI and cloud environments. When implemented effectively, they enable flexibility and productivity while maintaining strong protection. When neglected, they become a primary source of risk.

8.1 Zero Trust Principles and Identity Centric Security Models

As cloud and AI environments dissolve traditional boundaries, trust can no longer be assumed based on network location or system proximity. This shift has given rise to zero trust security models, which fundamentally redefine how access decisions are made. Zero trust is not a product or a single technology. It is a security philosophy built on the assumption that no user, device, or system should be trusted by default, regardless of where it resides.

In identity centric security models, identity becomes the primary signal for establishing trust. Every access request is evaluated based on who or what is making the request, the context in which it occurs, and the level of risk involved. This evaluation happens continuously rather than as a one-time decision at login. As a result, access is treated as a dynamic process rather than a static entitlement.

Zero trust principles emphasize continuous verification. Authentication and authorization are enforced at every stage of interaction. Even after initial access is granted, subsequent actions may be challenged or restricted if risk conditions change. This approach limits the damage that can occur if credentials are compromised or if a trusted system begins behaving unexpectedly.

Micro-segmentation is a key architectural component of zero trust models. Rather than granting broad access across networks or services, micro-segmentation restricts communication to what is explicitly required. In cloud environments, this may involve isolating workloads, limiting service to service communication, and enforcing granular access policies. Micro-segmentation reduces lateral movement and confines potential compromise to a narrow scope.

Artificial intelligence enhances zero trust by supporting adaptive decision making. AI systems analyze behavioral patterns, device posture, and historical activity to assess risk in real time. When anomalies are detected, access requirements can be adjusted dynamically. This may include prompting for additional authentication, limiting session duration, or restricting access to sensitive resources. AI driven adaptation allows zero trust models to respond intelligently rather than rigidly.

Zero trust also addresses the challenge of insider risk. Traditional security models often assume that internal users are trustworthy. In contrast, zero trust treats internal and external access consistently. This does not imply suspicion of all users, but rather recognition that risk can arise from compromised accounts, misuse, or error. By applying the same verification standards universally, zero trust reduces blind spots.

Implementing zero trust requires careful planning. Overly aggressive controls can disrupt productivity and create friction. Effective implementation balances security with usability by aligning controls with risk levels. Low risk interactions may proceed with minimal friction, while high risk situations trigger stronger safeguards. Clear communication with users helps ensure that controls are understood and accepted.

Governance plays an important role in zero trust adoption. Policies must define acceptable risk thresholds, authentication requirements, and enforcement mechanisms. These policies guide technical implementation and ensure consistency across systems. Without governance, zero trust efforts may become fragmented or inconsistently applied.

Zero trust is particularly relevant in environments where secure collaboration is essential. External partners, contractors, and cloud services often require access to internal resources. Zero trust models enable secure collaboration by granting access based on verified identity and context rather than network placement. This approach supports flexibility while maintaining strong protection.

As organizations continue to adopt AI and cloud technologies, zero trust principles provide a practical framework for managing access in complex environments. By centering security on identity and continuous verification, zero trust models address the realities of modern digital systems. This subheading establishes the conceptual foundation for deeper exploration of access enforcement, collaboration controls, and identity lifecycle management in the sections that follow.

8.2 Managing Non-Human Identities and Machine to Machine Access

As automation becomes central to cloud and AI systems, non-human identities have emerged as one of the most critical and least visible elements of cybersecurity. Non-human identities include service accounts, application identities, application programming interfaces, and automated agents that interact with systems without direct human involvement. These identities enable continuous operation and integration, but they also introduce significant security risk when not managed with the same discipline applied to human users.

Machine to machine access underpins modern digital infrastructure. Applications exchange data, trigger workflows, and invoke services automatically. In cloud environments, these interactions often occur at high frequency and scale. Non-human identities are typically granted broad privileges to ensure reliability and performance. However, excessive or poorly managed privileges make these identities attractive targets for attackers.

One challenge in managing non-human identities is visibility. Unlike human users, machine identities do not log in interactively or exhibit intuitive behavior. Their actions blend into normal system operations, making misuse difficult to detect. Without clear inventory and monitoring, organizations may not know how many non-human identities exist, what permissions they hold, or whether they are still required.

Lifecycle management is essential for securing machine identities. Non-human identities are often created during development or integration and then forgotten. Over time, unused or outdated identities accumulate, creating unnecessary exposure. Secure architectures enforce lifecycle controls that ensure machine identities are created deliberately, reviewed regularly, and decommissioned when no longer needed.

Access control for non-human identities should follow the same least privilege principles applied to human users. Permissions must be narrowly scoped and limited to specific resources and actions. Where possible, short lived credentials and token based authentication reduce the risk associated with long standing secrets. This approach limits the window of opportunity for attackers who obtain credentials.

Artificial intelligence can support the management of machine identities by analyzing usage patterns and detecting anomalies. For example, AI systems can identify when an application identity begins accessing resources outside its typical scope or operating at unusual times. These signals help security teams respond to potential compromise that might otherwise go unnoticed.

Secure collaboration between systems also depends on trust relationships. When services authenticate to one another, trust must be established through validated identities and secure channels. Mutual authentication mechanisms ensure that both parties verify each other before exchanging data. This reduces the risk of impersonation and unauthorized access.

Governance structures must explicitly address non-human identities. Policies that focus only on human access leave a significant gap in security posture. Governance frameworks should define standards for creating, managing, and auditing machine identities. Clear ownership ensures accountability for how these identities are used and protected.

Monitoring and auditing are critical for maintaining control over machine to machine access. Logs of service interactions, token usage, and permission changes provide visibility into automated activity. These logs support incident investigation and compliance reporting. Without auditing, misuse of non-human identities may persist undetected.

Managing non-human identities requires coordination between development, operations, and security teams. Developers often create machine identities to enable functionality, while security teams define acceptable controls. Collaboration ensures that automation supports both performance and protection. Clear guidelines help teams build secure integrations without unnecessary friction.

As cloud and AI systems continue to scale, non-human identities will outnumber human users by a wide margin. Securing these identities is therefore essential to maintaining control over distributed environments. By applying disciplined lifecycle management, least privilege access, and continuous monitoring, organizations can reduce risk while enabling the automation that modern systems depend on.

8.3 Identity Lifecycle Governance and Access Review Discipline

Effective identity and access control does not end with authentication and authorization. It requires continuous oversight of how identities evolve over time. Identity lifecycle governance refers to the structured management of identities from creation through modification to eventual removal. In cloud and AI environments where users, roles, and systems change frequently, lifecycle governance is essential to preventing access sprawl and hidden risk.

Identity creation is often driven by operational urgency. New employees join, contractors are onboarded, applications are deployed, and integrations are enabled. Without defined governance, identities may be created quickly without sufficient review. Secure systems enforce standardized onboarding processes that require justification, approval, and alignment with defined roles. This ensures that access is intentional rather than incidental.

As roles and responsibilities change, access requirements must evolve accordingly. One of the most common security failures in organizations is permission accumulation. Users and systems retain access long after it is needed. Over time, this accumulation creates excessive privilege that increases exposure. Lifecycle governance addresses this issue by linking access rights to current function rather than historical need.

Periodic access reviews are a core mechanism for enforcing lifecycle discipline. These reviews involve evaluating whether identities still require the permissions they hold. In cloud environments, where permissions can span multiple services and regions, access reviews must be systematic and supported by tooling. Manual reviews alone are insufficient at scale. Automation helps identify anomalies and highlight permissions that exceed defined baselines.

Artificial intelligence enhances access review processes by providing contextual insight. AI systems can analyze usage patterns to determine whether access rights are actively used and whether usage aligns with expected behavior. Permissions that are unused or rarely exercised may represent unnecessary risk. By highlighting such cases, AI supports more informed review decisions.

Deprovisioning is a critical but often neglected stage of the identity lifecycle. When users leave an organization or when systems are retired, access must be revoked promptly. Delayed deprovisioning leaves dormant accounts that can be exploited. Secure identity governance integrates deprovisioning with human resources and system management processes to ensure timely removal of access.

Machine identities require the same lifecycle discipline as human users. Service accounts and application identities must be reviewed regularly to confirm continued necessity. Automated systems that no longer serve an active purpose should be decommissioned. Without lifecycle governance, machine identities can persist indefinitely, creating long term exposure.

Lifecycle governance also supports compliance and audit readiness. Many regulatory frameworks require evidence that access is reviewed and controlled. Documented lifecycle processes and review outcomes demonstrate due diligence and accountability. In dynamic cloud environments, automated reporting and evidence collection simplify compliance and reduce administrative burden.

Governance frameworks must define ownership of identity lifecycle processes. Clear responsibility ensures that reviews are conducted consistently and that findings result in action. Without ownership, reviews may become perfunctory exercises that fail to reduce risk. Accountability reinforces the seriousness of access governance and encourages continuous improvement.

Cultural factors influence the effectiveness of lifecycle governance. Users and managers may resist access removal due to perceived inconvenience or future uncertainty. Clear communication about security objectives and risk helps build support for disciplined access management. When governance is understood as a protective measure rather than an obstacle, adoption improves.

Identity lifecycle governance is foundational to secure collaboration and access control. It ensures that access reflects current reality rather than outdated assumptions. By enforcing disciplined onboarding, review, and deprovisioning practices, organizations reduce hidden risk and strengthen trust in their security posture.

8.4 Balancing Security and Productivity in Collaborative Cloud Environments

One of the most delicate challenges in identity and access control is maintaining a balance between strong security and effective collaboration. Cloud platforms are designed to enable rapid sharing of data, tools, and services across teams and organizations. While this flexibility drives productivity, it also introduces risk when access controls are applied too loosely or enforced without clear structure. Achieving balance requires intentional design that supports collaboration while preserving security boundaries.

Security measures that are overly restrictive can slow work, frustrate users, and encourage workarounds. When users perceive security controls as obstacles, they may bypass approved processes by sharing credentials, using unauthorized tools, or duplicating data in insecure locations. These behaviors increase exposure and undermine governance objectives. Effective security therefore considers usability as a core design requirement rather than an afterthought.

Clear access models support both security and productivity. When users understand what access they have and why, friction is reduced. Role based access and contextual controls help ensure that collaboration is enabled where appropriate and restricted where risk is higher. This clarity reduces confusion and limits the need for ad hoc access requests.

Time bound access is a valuable tool in collaborative environments. Temporary access enables users to complete specific tasks without granting permanent privileges. When access expires automatically, the risk of accumulation is reduced. This approach is particularly effective for project based collaboration with external partners or cross functional teams.

Artificial intelligence can support balanced access decisions by assessing risk dynamically. Rather than applying static restrictions, AI systems evaluate behavior and context to adjust controls in real time. For example, collaboration may proceed normally under low risk conditions, while additional verification is required when anomalies are detected. This adaptive approach minimizes disruption while preserving protection.

Secure collaboration also depends on visibility. Users and administrators must be able to see who has access to shared resources and how those resources are used. Transparency builds trust and enables early detection of misuse. Cloud platforms offer tools for monitoring access and sharing activity, but these tools must be configured and actively used.

Governance frameworks should explicitly address collaborative scenarios. Policies that focus solely on internal access often fail to account for partnerships, contractors, and third party integrations. Clear guidelines for external collaboration define acceptable access models, data sharing practices, and approval requirements. These guidelines support consistent decision making and reduce uncertainty.

Training and awareness play an important role in balancing security and productivity. Users who understand security objectives are more likely to follow approved collaboration practices. Education helps users recognize risks associated with informal sharing and reinforces the importance of using secure tools. When users are empowered rather than constrained, compliance improves.

Leadership support is essential to sustaining balance. When leaders model secure behavior and prioritize both protection and productivity, teams are more likely to adopt disciplined practices. Leadership engagement signals that security is a shared responsibility rather than a technical burden.

Balancing security and productivity is not a one time achievement. It requires ongoing evaluation as tools, workflows, and risk conditions change. Regular feedback from users helps identify friction points and opportunities for improvement. Adaptive governance ensures that controls remain relevant and effective.

CHAPTER 9

MONITORING, VISIBILITY, AND INTELLIGENCE FOR CONTINUOUS SECURITY AWARENESS

Security awareness in modern digital environments is not achieved through isolated controls or periodic assessments. It is sustained through continuous monitoring, deep visibility, and actionable intelligence. As AI and cloud systems operate at scale and evolve rapidly, organizations must maintain an ongoing understanding of what is happening across their environments. Monitoring and intelligence provide the awareness needed to detect risk early, respond effectively, and make informed decisions.

Monitoring refers to the systematic collection of data about system activity, performance, and behavior. In cloud and AI environments, this data includes access logs, configuration changes, network activity, application events, and model behavior. Without comprehensive monitoring, security teams operate with limited insight and are forced to react to incidents after damage has occurred. Continuous monitoring enables early detection of anomalies and supports proactive defense.

Visibility is closely related to monitoring but extends beyond data collection. Visibility involves the ability to interpret monitoring data in context. It answers questions about what systems exist, how they are connected, who is accessing them, and how data flows across environments. In complex cloud architectures, visibility is often fragmented across tools and teams. Achieving unified visibility requires intentional integration and consistent data management.

Cloud environments introduce unique visibility challenges. Resources can be created and destroyed dynamically, and services may span multiple regions and providers. Without centralized oversight, shadow resources and unmanaged services can proliferate. Visibility tools must therefore track assets continuously and update inventories automatically. This dynamic awareness supports accurate risk assessment and effective governance.

Artificial intelligence systems add another layer of complexity to monitoring and visibility. AI driven decisions may influence system behavior, access control, or response actions. Monitoring must extend to AI inputs, outputs, and performance metrics. Understanding how models behave under different conditions is essential to maintaining trust and detecting unintended consequences.

Security intelligence transforms raw monitoring data into insight. Intelligence involves analyzing patterns, correlating events, and identifying trends that indicate risk. Rather than focusing on individual alerts, intelligence driven approaches examine how signals relate to one another over time. This broader perspective supports more accurate detection and reduces noise.

Threat intelligence is a key component of security intelligence. It includes information about known attack techniques, adversary behavior, and emerging risks. When integrated with internal monitoring data, threat intelligence provides context that enhances detection and prioritization. However, threat intelligence must be relevant and timely to be effective. Excessive or poorly curated intelligence can overwhelm teams and dilute focus.

Behavioral intelligence plays an important role in modern security awareness. By establishing baselines for normal behavior, organizations can detect deviations that may indicate compromise or misuse. AI driven behavioral analysis supports this approach by learning patterns across users, systems, and applications. These insights enable earlier detection of subtle threats that might otherwise go unnoticed.

Monitoring and intelligence also support incident response and investigation. Detailed logs and contextual information allow teams to reconstruct events, understand impact, and identify root causes. Without sufficient visibility, investigations become speculative and incomplete. Strong monitoring practices reduce response time and improve accuracy during high pressure situations.

Operational intelligence extends beyond security events to include system health and performance. Availability issues, misconfigurations, and resource constraints can introduce security risk if left unaddressed. Integrating operational and security monitoring provides a more holistic view of system state and supports resilient operations.

Governance frameworks should define expectations for monitoring and intelligence. This includes specifying what data is collected, how long it is retained, and who has access. Clear policies ensure that monitoring supports security objectives while respecting privacy and regulatory requirements. Transparency about monitoring practices builds trust with users and stakeholders.

Automation enhances the effectiveness of monitoring and intelligence. Automated data collection, correlation, and alerting reduce reliance on manual processes and enable real time awareness. When automation is guided by clear thresholds and oversight, it improves consistency and scalability.

Human expertise remains essential. Analysts interpret intelligence, refine detection logic, and make contextual decisions that automation alone cannot. Effective security awareness combines machine driven analysis with human judgment. Training and experience enable teams to distinguish between noise and genuine risk.

Continuous improvement is a defining characteristic of effective monitoring and intelligence. Threat landscapes evolve, systems change, and new risks emerge. Monitoring strategies must adapt accordingly. Regular review of detection performance, false positives, and missed incidents supports ongoing refinement.

Monitoring, visibility, and intelligence form the nervous system of AI and cloud security architecture. They provide the awareness needed to navigate complexity and uncertainty. By maintaining continuous insight into system behavior and risk, organizations can move from reactive defense to informed, proactive security management.

9.1 Centralized Visibility and the Challenge of Security Data Fragmentation

One of the most significant obstacles to effective monitoring and intelligence in cloud and AI environments is fragmentation of security data. Modern systems generate information across many platforms, services, and tools. Logs may reside in different cloud accounts, regions, and applications. Security alerts may be produced by multiple detection systems that do not share context. Without centralized visibility, security teams struggle to form a coherent understanding of system behavior and risk.

Data fragmentation weakens security awareness by obscuring relationships between events. An authentication anomaly detected by an identity system may appear unrelated to a configuration change recorded elsewhere. Network activity, application logs, and AI model behavior may each tell part of a story, but without integration, that story remains incomplete. Attackers often exploit this lack of correlation by spreading activity across systems in ways that avoid triggering alarms in any single tool.

Centralized visibility addresses this challenge by aggregating security relevant data into a unified view. This does not require replacing all existing tools. Rather, it involves integrating data sources so that events can be analyzed collectively. Centralized visibility enables correlation across domains, revealing patterns that would otherwise remain hidden.

Cloud environments make centralized visibility both more necessary and more complex. Resources are dynamic, and services scale automatically. Visibility systems must adapt to this dynamism by discovering assets continuously and updating data flows accordingly. Static inventories and manual integration quickly become outdated in such environments.

Artificial intelligence plays an important role in managing centralized visibility at scale. AI driven analytics can process large volumes of heterogeneous data, identify relationships, and surface meaningful insights. By filtering noise and highlighting significant patterns, AI helps security teams focus on what matters most. However, AI depends on comprehensive and accurate data. Fragmentation reduces its effectiveness.

Governance considerations also shape centralized visibility. Data collection must respect privacy requirements and regulatory constraints. Policies must define what data is collected, how it is stored, and who can access it. Transparency about monitoring practices supports trust and compliance while enabling security awareness.

Centralized visibility improves more than threat detection. It supports operational resilience, compliance reporting, and strategic planning. By understanding how systems behave over time, organizations can identify systemic weaknesses and prioritize improvements. Visibility becomes a foundation for informed decision making rather than a reactive capability.

Case Study: Overcoming Fragmented Visibility in a Multi Cloud Environment

A large organization operating across multiple cloud providers faced persistent challenges related to security visibility. Each business unit managed its own cloud accounts and monitoring tools. Logs were collected locally, and alerts were reviewed by separate teams. While individual tools functioned adequately, there was no unified view of security activity across the organization.

During a routine investigation, security analysts discovered inconsistencies between access logs and configuration records across different environments. The lack of centralized visibility made it difficult to determine whether these inconsistencies represented benign variation or coordinated malicious activity. Investigations were slow and often inconclusive due to missing context.

To address this issue, the organization implemented a centralized security data platform that aggregated logs, alerts, and configuration data from all cloud environments. Standard data formats were adopted to support correlation, and asset discovery processes were automated to maintain an accurate inventory. Access to the centralized platform was governed by strict role based controls.

Once centralized visibility was established, analysts were able to correlate identity events with network activity and configuration changes across environments. Patterns that had previously gone unnoticed became visible. For example, repeated access anomalies across different cloud providers were linked to a single compromised integration account. Early detection prevented further spread and limited impact.

The organization also benefited from improved compliance reporting. Centralized records simplified audit preparation and reduced manual effort. Over time, security teams shifted from reactive investigation to proactive risk identification based on observed trends.

9.2 From Raw Data to Actionable Intelligence in AI Driven Security Operations

Collecting large volumes of security data does not automatically lead to better security outcomes. In many organizations, monitoring systems generate far more information than security teams can reasonably analyze. Logs, alerts, metrics, and reports accumulate continuously, yet meaningful insight remains elusive. The challenge lies not in data availability, but in transforming raw data into actionable intelligence that supports timely and effective decision making.

Actionable intelligence is information that provides clear guidance on what action to take, why it is necessary, and what impact it may have. It bridges the gap between observation and response. Without this transformation, security teams may become overwhelmed, leading to delayed responses or missed threats. AI driven security operations address this challenge by applying analytics and context to raw data, enabling prioritization and clarity.

Artificial intelligence supports this transformation by identifying patterns and relationships that are difficult for humans to detect manually. Machine learning models analyze historical incidents, behavioral trends, and environmental context to assess risk. Rather than presenting hundreds of isolated alerts, AI systems surface a smaller number of high confidence insights that warrant attention. This reduction in noise improves efficiency and decision quality.

Context is essential to actionable intelligence. An event that appears suspicious in isolation may be harmless when considered alongside business activity, system role, or time of occurrence. AI systems incorporate contextual factors such as asset criticality, user role, and operational state to evaluate significance. This contextualization ensures that intelligence reflects real risk rather than abstract anomalies.

Prioritization is another critical aspect of intelligence driven operations. Not all risks carry equal impact. AI systems rank threats based on likelihood and potential consequence, enabling teams to allocate resources effectively. This prioritization supports strategic decision making and reduces the tendency to focus on low impact issues simply because they are visible.

Explainability strengthens the value of actionable intelligence. Security teams must understand why a particular insight is generated in order to trust and act on it. AI driven systems that provide reasoning, contributing factors, and confidence levels support informed response. Without explainability, intelligence may be ignored or questioned, undermining its effectiveness.

Actionable intelligence also supports proactive defense. By identifying trends and emerging patterns, organizations can address vulnerabilities before they are exploited. This may include strengthening controls, adjusting access policies, or refining monitoring thresholds. Proactive action reduces reliance on incident driven response and improves overall resilience.

Case Study: Enhancing Security Operations Through Intelligence Driven Prioritization

A technology organization operating a cloud based platform faced growing pressure on its security operations team. Monitoring tools generated a high volume of alerts daily, many of which required manual review. Despite significant effort, response times for serious incidents were inconsistent, and analysts reported fatigue and frustration.

To address this challenge, the organization implemented an AI driven intelligence layer on top of its existing monitoring infrastructure. The system ingested alerts, logs, and contextual data from across the environment. Machine learning models assessed historical outcomes and behavioral patterns to rank alerts by risk.

Within weeks, the number of alerts requiring immediate attention decreased significantly. Low risk events were deprioritized automatically, while high confidence indicators were surfaced prominently. Each prioritized alert included contextual information explaining why it was considered significant, such as affected assets, unusual behavior patterns, and potential impact.

One incident involved abnormal data access activity within a non-critical system. Traditional rules flagged the activity as moderate risk. The AI system elevated its priority based on correlation with recent credential anomalies and access timing. Analysts investigated promptly and discovered early stage compromise linked to a third party integration. Containment occurred before sensitive systems were affected.

Over time, the security operations team reported improved focus and confidence in decision making. Response times improved, and collaboration with other teams became more effective due to clearer communication of risk. The organization also gained insight into recurring patterns that informed improvements to architecture and policy.

CHAPTER 10

BUILDING A FUTURE READY SECURITY POSTURE FOR AI AND CLOUD ENVIRONMENTS

Security has always evolved alongside technology, but the pace of change introduced by artificial intelligence and cloud computing has reshaped what it means to be secure. Organizations no longer operate within stable, predictable environments. Systems scale dynamically, decisions are automated, and digital interactions span borders and platforms. In this context, a future ready security posture is not defined by static controls or compliance checklists. It is defined by adaptability, intelligence, and sustained alignment between technology, governance, and human judgment.

A future ready security posture begins with acceptance of uncertainty. Threat landscapes change continuously, and new technologies introduce unforeseen risks. Attempting to predict every possible threat is neither practical nor effective. Instead, organizations must focus on building capabilities that allow them to detect change early, respond decisively, and recover quickly. This mindset shifts security from a defensive stance to a strategic function that supports long term resilience.

Artificial intelligence will continue to play an expanding role in cybersecurity. As systems generate more data than humans can analyze manually, AI driven analytics will become essential for maintaining visibility and awareness. However, future readiness requires thoughtful integration of AI rather than uncritical adoption. Organizations must ensure that AI systems are transparent, governed, and aligned with ethical and regulatory expectations. Trust in automated systems is built through oversight, validation, and accountability.

Cloud platforms will remain central to digital transformation. Their flexibility and scale offer significant advantages, but they also demand disciplined security architecture. Future ready organizations treat cloud security as a design principle rather than an operational afterthought. Secure deployment patterns, identity centric access control, and continuous monitoring are embedded into how systems are built and maintained. This approach reduces reliance on reactive fixes and supports sustainable growth.

One of the most important lessons from modern security practice is that technology alone cannot deliver resilience. Human factors remain critical. Decision making under pressure, ethical judgment, and cross functional collaboration shape security outcomes. Future ready security programs invest in people as much as in tools. Training, clear communication, and leadership engagement ensure that security is understood as a shared responsibility rather than a specialized function.

Governance will continue to define the boundaries within which security operates. As regulations evolve and public expectations around data protection and AI use increase, organizations must maintain adaptable governance frameworks. These frameworks should support innovation while enforcing accountability. Clear roles, documented decision processes, and continuous review help organizations navigate complexity without losing control.

Risk management in future ready organizations is continuous rather than periodic. Static assessments quickly become outdated in dynamic environments. Instead, risk is evaluated in real time using monitoring data, behavioral intelligence, and contextual insight. This continuous approach enables organizations to adjust priorities as conditions change and to allocate resources where they are most needed.

Resilience remains the ultimate measure of security effectiveness. Future ready systems are designed to withstand disruption without catastrophic failure. They isolate risk, degrade gracefully, and recover efficiently. This resilience is reinforced through regular testing, simulation, and learning. Organizations that treat incidents as opportunities for improvement strengthen their security posture over time.

Collaboration will increasingly shape security outcomes. As ecosystems expand to include partners, vendors, and third party services, trust relationships must be managed carefully. Secure collaboration frameworks enable organizations to work effectively across boundaries without exposing critical assets. Identity based access, clear governance, and shared standards support this balance.

Ethical considerations will become more prominent as AI driven systems influence decisions that affect individuals and societies. Future ready security programs incorporate ethical review into system design and operation. Transparency, fairness, and respect for privacy are not optional enhancements. They are essential to maintaining legitimacy and trust.

Looking ahead, the organizations that succeed will be those that view security as an enabler of progress rather than a barrier to innovation. By aligning security with business objectives, organizations can move faster with confidence. Security becomes a foundation for trust, supporting new services, partnerships, and opportunities.

This work has explored the principles, strategies, and frameworks needed to protect AI powered and cloud based systems in an evolving threat landscape. From foundational concepts to advanced defense mechanisms, the central theme has remained consistent. Effective security is adaptive, integrated, and human centered.

The digital frontier will continue to expand. New technologies will emerge, and new risks will follow. Organizations cannot control the pace of change, but they can control how prepared they are to face it. A future ready security posture does not promise perfect protection. It promises readiness, resilience, and the capacity to evolve. In embracing this posture, organizations position themselves not only to defend against threats, but to thrive in a world defined by intelligence, connectivity, and constant transformation.

10.1 Embedding Security as a Continuous Organizational Capability

A future ready security posture cannot exist as a standalone program or a periodic initiative. It must be embedded into the organization as a continuous capability that evolves alongside technology, business strategy, and societal expectations. This embedding represents a shift from viewing security as a function to viewing it as an organizational trait. When security becomes intrinsic to how decisions are made and systems are designed, resilience emerges naturally rather than through constant intervention.

Embedding security begins with integration into organizational workflows. Security considerations must be present at every stage of system development and operation. In cloud and AI environments, this includes architecture design, model development, deployment pipelines, and operational monitoring. When security is integrated early, it becomes easier to manage and less disruptive. Late stage security controls often introduce friction because they attempt to constrain systems that were not designed with protection in mind.

Leadership commitment is central to embedding security as a capability. Leaders influence priorities, resource allocation, and organizational culture. When leadership treats security as a strategic concern rather than a technical cost, teams are more likely to adopt disciplined practices. This commitment must be visible through consistent messaging, investment in capability building, and accountability for security outcomes.

Organizational structure also influences how security is embedded. Future ready organizations avoid isolating security within a single department. Instead, security expertise is distributed across teams through shared responsibility models. Developers, data scientists, operations staff, and business leaders each play a role in maintaining security. Central security teams provide guidance, oversight, and coordination, but protection is enacted collectively.

Measurement supports continuous capability development. Organizations must move beyond simple metrics such as incident counts or compliance status. Meaningful indicators include response effectiveness, resilience under stress, and the ability to adapt controls as conditions change. These metrics reflect how security functions in practice rather than how they appear on paper.

Learning is another essential component of embedded security. Incidents, near misses, and operational disruptions provide valuable insight into system behavior. Organizations that capture and apply these lessons strengthen their security posture over time. This learning process must be systematic rather than ad hoc. Structured reviews, knowledge sharing, and continuous improvement initiatives reinforce adaptive capability.

Technology supports embedding but does not replace human engagement. Automated controls, AI driven analytics, and cloud native security tools enhance efficiency and scale. However, these tools are only effective when used within a culture that values responsibility and awareness. Training and professional development ensure that teams understand not only how systems work, but why security matters.

Embedding security also requires alignment with organizational values. Decisions about data use, AI deployment, and collaboration have ethical and social implications. Future ready organizations consider these implications as part of security planning. This alignment strengthens trust with customers, partners, and regulators and reinforces legitimacy in an increasingly scrutinized digital landscape.

As environments grow more complex, the cost of fragmented or superficial security increases. Organizations that embed security as a continuous capability reduce reliance on crisis response and external enforcement. They gain confidence in their ability to operate responsibly under uncertainty.

10.2 Preparing for Emerging Threats and the Next Generation of Digital Risk

Future ready security requires more than responding to known threats. It demands deliberate preparation for risks that have not yet fully materialized. As artificial intelligence, cloud computing, and digital ecosystems continue to evolve, new forms of vulnerability will emerge alongside opportunity. Organizations that prepare proactively are better positioned to manage uncertainty and maintain trust in an increasingly interconnected world.

Emerging threats often arise at the intersection of technologies rather than within a single domain. AI systems may introduce new attack surfaces through data poisoning, model manipulation, or unintended behavior. Cloud platforms may amplify the impact of misconfiguration or dependency failure due to their scale and interconnectedness. Preparing for these risks requires holistic thinking that considers how systems interact rather than how they function in isolation.

Adversaries are also evolving. Threat actors increasingly leverage automation, intelligence, and scale. Attacks may unfold slowly and subtly rather than through obvious disruption. This shift challenges traditional detection models that focus on known signatures or isolated events. Future ready security programs invest in behavioral analysis, anomaly detection, and long term pattern recognition to identify emerging threats early.

Strategic foresight is an important capability in preparing for future risk. This involves monitoring technological trends, regulatory developments, and changes in adversary behavior. By engaging in horizon scanning and scenario planning, organizations can explore potential futures and assess how current controls may perform under different conditions. This proactive approach supports informed investment and reduces surprise.

Resilience planning must also account for systemic risk. As organizations rely more heavily on shared platforms and global services, disruptions can propagate rapidly. Preparing for such scenarios requires coordination across technical, operational, and leadership functions. Business continuity and security planning should be integrated to ensure that response strategies address both protection and recovery.

Ethical and societal considerations will increasingly shape the threat landscape. Public concern around data use, automated decision making, and surveillance continues to grow. Regulatory scrutiny is likely to intensify. Future ready organizations anticipate these concerns by designing systems that respect privacy, transparency, and fairness. Ethical foresight becomes a component of risk management rather than a separate exercise.

Investment in adaptability is critical. Fixed security architectures struggle to keep pace with change. Modular designs, flexible policies, and continuous learning enable organizations to adjust as conditions evolve. This adaptability reduces the cost of change and supports sustained security effectiveness.

Collaboration across sectors will play a greater role in addressing emerging threats. No organization operates in isolation. Information sharing, joint standards, and cooperative response efforts strengthen collective defense. Trust based collaboration enhances situational awareness and accelerates learning across the broader ecosystem.

Preparing for the future also involves cultivating talent. Security professionals must develop skills that extend beyond technical expertise. Understanding AI behavior, regulatory implications, and organizational dynamics becomes increasingly important. Continuous professional development ensures that teams can navigate complexity with confidence.

REFERENCES

Anderson, R. (2020). Security engineering: A guide to building dependable distributed systems (3rd ed.). Wiley.

Behl, A., Pereira, V., & Del Giudice, M. (2022). Artificial intelligence and cyber defense: A systematic review and future research agenda. Technological Forecasting and Social Change, 174, 121246. https://doi.org/10.1016/j.techfore.2021.121246

Bishop, M. (2019). Computer security: Art and science (2nd ed.). Addison-Wesley.

Cloud Security Alliance. (2023). Security guidance for critical areas of focus in cloud computing v5.0. Cloud Security Alliance. https://cloudsecurityalliance.org

ENISA. (2021). Artificial intelligence cybersecurity challenges. European Union Agency for Cybersecurity. https://www.enisa.europa.eu

Gartner. (2023). Hype cycle for security operations. Gartner Research.

Goodfellow, I., Bengio, Y., & Courville, A. (2016). Deep learning. MIT Press.

ISO/IEC. (2022). ISO/IEC 27001:2022 Information security, cybersecurity and privacy protection. International Organization for Standardization.

ISO/IEC. (2023). ISO/IEC 27017:2023 Code of practice for information security controls for cloud services. International Organization for Standardization.

Kindervag, J. (2010). Build security into your network's DNA: The zero trust network architecture. Forrester Research.

Kumar, R., Khan, A. A., Abushark, Y. B., Alam, M. M., Agrawal, A., & Khan, R. A. (2022). Cybersecurity challenges in cloud computing: A review. IEEE Access, 10, 103707–103720. https://doi.org/10.1109/ACCESS.2022.3201531

National Institute of Standards and Technology. (2020). Security and privacy controls for information systems and organizations (SP 800-53 Rev. 5). NIST. https://doi.org/10.6028/NIST.SP.800-53r5

National Institute of Standards and Technology. (2021). Zero trust architecture (SP 800-207). NIST. https://doi.org/10.6028/NIST.SP.800-207

National Institute of Standards and Technology. (2023). Artificial intelligence risk management framework (AI RMF 1.0). NIST. https://www.nist.gov

Pearson, S. (2013). Privacy, security and trust in cloud computing. Privacy and Security for Cloud Computing, 3–42. Springer.

Shameli-Sendi, A., Aghababaei-Barzegar, R., & Cheriet, M. (2016). Taxonomy of information security risk assessment (ISRA). Computers & Security, 57, 14–30. https://doi.org/10.1016/j.cose.2015.11.001

Sivarajah, U., Irani, Z., Gupta, S., & Mahroof, K. (2020). Role of big data and artificial intelligence in cybersecurity. International Journal of Information Management, 54, 102168. https://doi.org/10.1016/j.ijinfomgt.2020.102168

Sommer, R., & Paxson, V. (2010). Outside the closed world: On using machine learning for network intrusion detection. IEEE Symposium on Security and Privacy, 305–316. https://doi.org/10.1109/SP.2010.25

Zhang, Q., Chen, M., Li, L., & Li, X. (2021). AI-driven cyber defense: Opportunities and challenges. IEEE Network, 35(4), 278–284. https://doi.org/10.1109/MNET.011.2000556

www.ingramcontent.com/pod-product-compliance
Lightning Source LLC
Chambersburg PA
CBHW051354240926
51852CB00001B/20
* 9 7 8 3 8 3 6 8 4 4 9 6 3 *